# CLOSE READING
## FOR THE WHOLE CLASS

Sandra K. Athans & Denise Ashe Devine

**SCHOLASTIC**

New York • Toronto • London • Auckland • Sydney
Mexico City • New Delhi • Hong Kong • Buenos Aires

# Acknowledgments

We are particularly thankful to the following:

- The very skilled group of editors, production staff, and marketing mavericks at Scholastic—they are an unparalleled group!
- Those theorists, authorities, pioneers, and practitioners who provided us with a solid foundation and encouraged us, through the simple act of sharing their expertise, to proceed in the right direction
- Our colleagues, within our district and beyond, who enthusiastically participated in our studies and provided us with invaluable data, anecdotes, and information, and to whom we remain grateful
- The Chittenango Central School District, including our administrators and board members, who maintain an unwavering commitment to education
- Finally, our readers—and your remarkable "can-do" attitude—we are deeply honored!

# Dedication

We dedicate this book to our students, whose enthusiasm for learning inspires us; to our colleagues, whose passion and talent for teaching are essential to our work; to our administration, whose support and encouragement enable us to share our ideas with others; and to our families, whose endless love and understanding make this all possible. We are truly one part of a great team!

Cover design: Jorge J. Namerow
Interior design: Teresa B. Southwell
Interior photographs: Sandra K. Athans and Denise Ashe Devine
Development Editor: Joanna Davis-Swing
Production Editor: Sarah Glasscock
Copy Editor: David Klein

ISBN: 978-0-545-62676-7
Copyright © 2015 by Sandra K. Athans and Denise Ashe Devine

All rights reserved. Published by Scholastic Inc.
Printed in the U.S.A.
1 2 3 4 5 6 7 8 9 10    40    22 21 20 19 18 17 16 15

# Contents

# ⌕ Introduction

We are practicing teachers. The daily work we do in our integrated classrooms is a scramble. Our class sizes are growing, our technology and book budgets are shrinking, and our students' needs are expanding in diverse directions. The daily tugs on our attention and energy often leave us breathless. Yet these challenges are symptomatic of the times. These are the struggles felt by all classroom teachers today, and they can be very overwhelming!

The good news is that through our use of close reading as part of a balanced literacy approach, we have made some incredible gains! Our students are reading grade-level materials deeply and analytically, and they are improving at meeting high expectations, such as those of the Common Core State Standards (CCSS). This is true within all five of our district's fourth-grade classrooms and beyond. As nearly 40 percent of the students in our economically diverse population are eligible for free or reduced lunches, and roughly a quarter of the learners in every classroom meet criteria for remedial reading services, this is quite an achievement.

## Case Study: Changing Small-Group Instruction—Our Journey

Of the many standards-initiated changes we have introduced into our classrooms, adopting close reading as a primary method of reading instruction is one of the most significant. Prior to this, our reading approach resembled what many teachers nationwide were doing: small-group, differentiated instruction. We placed students into homogenous groups based on their shared reading abilities and guided their instruction using leveled materials. Meeting routinely with three to five reading groups, we taught well-known reading comprehension strategies and had students refine their grasp of these strategies. Our guided lessons focused on asking questions, making predictions, finding the main idea, and other strategies that represent the authentic behaviors of good readers. We considered small-group, strategy-based, guided-reading instruction a best practice, whose benefits were supported by extensive research.

Although our students benefited from this instruction for many years, their success began to wane at roughly the same time as the new Common Core State Standards were rolled out. We were concerned that our students' declining performance supported our larger suspicion—their needs were growing and changing and our efforts to help them were no longer keeping pace.

Likewise, we were baffled by our New York State Education Commissioner's strategy of encouraging all students to read grade-level materials, which we teachers were to support through the use of close reading. This struck us as counterproductive to our objective of instilling a love of reading and presented a serious challenge to our struggling readers. Thankfully, we forged a model of instruction that allowed us to meet the academic rigor of the standards and also help our struggling learners. Close reading is a significant component of this model—and the focus of our book.

⌘

In these pages you'll find the following:

- Proven tactics to make your classroom close reading highly beneficial to all students, no matter which standards your district uses
- Mind-set shifts—positive ways to rethink some former practices
- Tips for successfully implementing each close reading component into your classroom
- Classroom-ready materials to use as is or to adapt

We've also included professional development activities at the end of each chapter that will help you further explore the chapter topics. These activities can be used flexibly for formal study, such as with Professional Learning Communities (PLCs), or for small study groups or independent work.

**Note:** We want to stress that although we sometimes refer to the CCSS, the information presented here will help you develop close reading skills no matter which standards your state or district uses. You can download a copy of the CCSS from www.corestandards.org/ELA-Literacy to use as you read this book.

The material presented here can be used for students in grades 2 through 6. We carefully and purposefully selected these grade levels because of critical threads we detected across the continuum of standards at these levels. For example, students are expected to grasp key details more broadly beginning in grade 2. Also, students' knowledge of the importance of author intention, point of view, and text structure takes root at grade 2 and then builds and broadens across subsequent grade levels. At the other end of the range, grade 6 has some noteworthy features in terms of the CCSS. One of the most significant is the introduction of the literacy standards in history/social science, science, and technical subjects.

Recognizing and addressing the standards' usefulness in complementing content-area instruction across all grade levels is critical. We share ways for modifying strategies for text selection, creating text-dependent questions, and teaching close reading skills to address the grade-level needs of your students. Here's an overview of the contents of each chapter:

**Chapter 1, Introduction to Close Reading,** describes close reading basics in teacher-friendly terms. Whether you've already begun to implement close reading in your classroom or you're looking for ways to hone your close reading savvy, the fundamentals in this chapter will prove helpful.

**Chapter 2, Lesson Design and Delivery,** explains what close reading looks like in a classroom. This includes the design of lessons as well as the manner in which instruction can be delivered. We explain why our emphasis on close reading has proven effective and also share an overview of the flexible plan we use to guide our daily reading instruction.

**Chapter 3, Text Selection,** presents the nuts and bolts of selecting appropriate texts to use for close reading. Even if your district has adopted a reading program and/or other assembled reading materials, you'll want to explore ways to untangle the features of text complexity and deliver your lessons with finesse whether you're using informational text or literature.

**Chapter 4, Text-Dependent Questions,** steers you toward creating highly effective questions that scaffold student learning *and* encourage deep and thoughtful analysis of text passages. Developing a keen ability to devise, adapt, and use questions skillfully and effectively is critical to the success of your close reading instruction. This is true whether you select your own materials or use preassembled materials.

**Chapter 5, Performance Tasks,** features guidelines for creating tasks that are efficient on two fronts: (1) tasks that help enrich students' understanding of a passage and (2) tasks that enable students to demonstrate to others the degree to which they've grasped the content of a passage.

**Chapter 6, Academic Discussions,** shows how to rev up your existing classroom discussion practices to better support and enhance close reading instruction. Today, classroom discussion is an invaluable instructional asset. With these discussions, you can help students build complex ideas cohesively, wield evidence effectively, and communicate ideas clearly.

**Chapter 7, Close Read Guides: A Nifty Tool For Instruction,** describes how to combine all the components of a close reading lesson into a user-friendly guide for you and your students. Easy-to-follow steps outline how to organize theme-based units and construct your own guides.

**Chapter 8, Nitty-Gritty Strategies and Take-5 Mini-Lessons for Close Reading,** features classroom-tested strategies that will prove helpful as you launch and master the delivery of your close reading instruction. Sample Take-5 Mini-Lessons demonstrate how to introduce some of these strategies. Suggestions for how to create mini-lessons for other strategies are also included.

⌘

Although our success in using close reading began with a core team of seven classroom teachers and reading specialists, it quickly spread to other grade levels in our district, and beyond. Teachers across the country reached out to us during conferences or workshops where we presented our ideas and they, in turn, adopted, reshaped, and shared these ideas. This teacher-to-teacher troubleshooting network is truly a marvel in action.

Still, our successes did not come easily. To varying degrees, we all had to change. And change is never easy. In this book, we share with you the shared voices of a swift and steadfast network of teachers who have piloted the success of close reading. Our motto, "Use this as you wish," continues to ring in the spirit of this collective teacher voice.

We have made significant gains. Like our students, we have rolled up our sleeves, dug deep down to the nitty-gritty, and we have come out champions—all of us!

# Introduction to Close Reading

Ask any five educators to define the term "close reading" and, no doubt, you'll get five different answers! Adding to the confusion, the term is used in teacher resources and educational literature as a noun, a verb, and an adjective. It is also a homophone and can easily be mistaken for "cloze reading," a well-known comprehension technique, which muddies things even more. It's no wonder we have trouble understanding what close reading is and, in turn, how to implement it in our classrooms!

Even though close reading has become a kind of melting pot of ideas—a fondue of fresh literacy beginnings—most literacy specialists agree that the following components are key: rich grade-level texts, reading and rereading deeply, seeking evidence to support ideas, acknowledging the author's intentions, and paying attention to text structure. Together with the specialists' shared ideas and our scrutiny of the standards and other available resources, we arrived at a definition that is simple, unambiguous, and classroom ready. Our teacher-friendly definition, discussed below, continues to steer us in the right direction.

## A Teacher-Friendly Definition and Description of Close Reading

Close reading means reading a passage very attentively, being mindful of its content, structure, and value. It is a deep, analytical method in which readers construct meaning based on the author's intention. Readers deduce this from evidence they glean from the text, such as identifying the key ideas or the position an author emphasizes, evaluating his or her word choice, and determining how an author organizes sentences and paragraphs to support an idea.

Close reading requires multiple steps, including the following:

- Deconstructing or breaking apart pieces of texts
- Examining the pieces carefully through repeated readings
- Carefully considering the meaning of each piece and how it contributes to the text as a whole
- Integrating this new knowledge in meaningful ways

Readers gauge their success with this process by evaluating how well their ideas square with the text-based evidence. Ensuring that their comprehension matches what the author most likely intended in the passage is key. Close reading enables readers to gain insights that surpass a cursory reading.

### The Non-Negotiables of Rigorous Reading

In creating our teacher-friendly definition of close reading, we carefully reviewed several sources: the CCSS, the ideas and research of literacy specialists, the resources provided by our New York State Education Department, literacy organizations, such as the International Reading Association, and other publishers classified as "official providers" of standards-based materials. A list of these resources begins on page 128.

In our review process, we noted critical characteristics of rigorous reading as outlined by the CCSS. Some we classified as "non-negotiables," meaning requirements that appear directly in the standards or in standards supplements and are referred to as "shifts," "crosswalks," "bridges," "progressions," and other state-designated terms that serve to distinguish their importance. The chart below shows these non-negotiables and the ways in which close reading addresses them.

## Non-Negotiable Characteristics of Rigorous Reading in the CCSS

| Characteristics of Rigorous Reading | Using Close Reading |
| --- | --- |
| Students read complex, grade-level text. | Instructional materials align with students' grade level and fall within a specific text complexity band.<br><br>All students work with complex, grade-level texts, rather than varied-level texts and reading groups. |
| Texts represent a balance of literature and informational works. | Text is carefully chosen to span a range of genres within a balanced collection of fiction and nonfiction. |
| Works of literature must include texts from diverse cultures. | Teacher provides a range of texts to meet the required standards. |
| Informational texts must include historical, scientific, and technical subjects. | Textbooks and other content-area materials may be used for reading instruction. |
| Students must demonstrate understanding by answering questions about key ideas and details. | Students are required to apply their sequencing, summarizing, comparing and contrasting skills, and other basic reading proficiencies.<br><br>Questions are carefully crafted to elicit evidence-based responses. |
| Students must support their ideas using text-based evidence. | Responses move beyond "finding details" and require that students provide evidence-based responses, including evidence to support inferences. |
| Craft and structure is a focus of instruction. | Students are required to apply their knowledge of vocabulary, literary technique, organizational structure, and their competency with key reading comprehension strategies.<br><br>More attention is paid to craft and structure than in previous instruction. |

*Close Reading for the Whole Class* • © 2015 by Sandra K. Athans & Denise Ashe Devine • Scholastic Teaching Resources

| | |
|---|---|
| Students focus on integrating features from a text or multiple texts. | Students must use their skills to interpret and evaluate text features, such as graphs, maps, charts, and animations, or to integrate information from multiple texts. |
| Students must read grade-level texts proficiently and independently by the end of the school year. | Students are provided with repeated opportunities to practice and refine close reading skills so they can comprehend grade-level material. |

## Pertinent Practices for Close Reading Instruction

In addition to noting these non-negotiables, we share other pertinent practices that were instrumental to the success of our start-up close reading instruction. We gleaned these from exemplary close reading lessons and other instructional materials on the website of our state education department. Collectively, these resources helped us grasp the components of an effective close reading lesson and also described a reading routine to deliver the close reading instruction.

- Teacher delivers lessons to the whole class.
- Teacher selects short, content-rich passages that enable students to delve deeply into the text in a timely and manageable manner.
- Teacher questions students about a text to determine how well they understand their reading and/or have mastered a skill, as well as to scaffold students' grasp of key ideas.
- These questions are "text-dependent." They require students to refer back directly to the text and do not require any background or experiential knowledge to be answered.
- Teacher also uses tasks, which are often deeper-level prompted inquiries, to determine how well students understand a text and/or the degree to which a skill has been mastered, as well as to help students comprehend key ideas.
- Students silently read the text independently, and then the teacher reads the text aloud as students follow along. Rereading occurs at intervals throughout the instruction and supports deeper analysis.
- Giving students opportunities to demonstrate their understanding, application of a skill, or knowledge orally and in writing provides some flexibility during instruction.
- Discussion supports students as they explore and analyze ideas.

From our tried-and-tested practice with the non-negotiables and pertinent practices, we devised the short list of essentials on the next page. Representing the core components of close reading instruction, these are the ingredients that, when mixed together carefully, will result in masterful close reading instruction that helps all students meet the standards more proficiently.

With these essentials, we can address most of the non-negotiable requirements of the standards as well as the preferential instructional practices.

- **Lesson design and delivery** help us define our whole-class approach and deliver grade-level instruction to all students. This is markedly different from the instructional approach we had in place prior to the national standards, which was small-group differentiated instruction using leveled texts. (See Case Study: Changing Small-Group Instruction—Our Journey on page 4.)

- **Text selection** ensures that the materials we use for instruction comply with CCSS complexity-band levels. We are also mindful of the length of the passages, the balance of literature and informational texts we select, and the content of the texts.

- **Text-dependent questions** help us determine if students are meeting the standards. We can also scaffold students' understanding as they think through complex ideas or challenging content of rich and worthwhile texts.

- **Performance tasks** allow us to monitor student success in meeting the standards and also help scaffold their understanding. As an added benefit, we can incorporate writing instruction into our reading instruction by including tasks that call for written responses.

- **Academic discussions** are shaped in a manner that best supports our close reading instruction. They serve as a forum to help students verbally grapple with challenging ideas. This process enables students to help one another build understanding through peer scaffolding, and we incorporate speaking and listening skill instruction into our reading instruction.

We have organized this book to reflect the importance of these essentials, each of which has its own chapter, yet is woven with the others into a cohesive approach to close reading instruction. You will also see how these essentials reflect the standards so you can be absolutely certain that your instruction is standard-aligned.

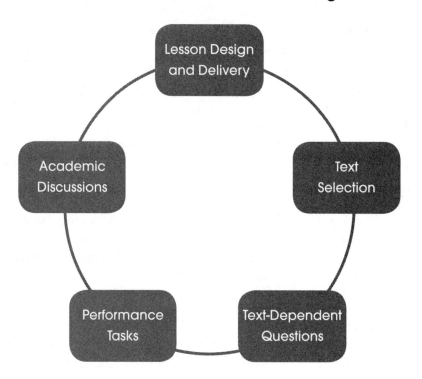

**The Essentials of Close Reading**

Lesson Design and Delivery

Text Selection

Text-Dependent Questions

Performance Tasks

Academic Discussions

# *Five Tips* for Introducing Close Reading Into Your Classroom

1.  **Don't assume that you're already doing close reading.** Even though your knowledge, practices, and classroom skills reflect your sincere intentions to help your students achieve success, you may not be using close reading to its full potential. Remember that close reading addresses the rigors of a deeper understanding of grade-level texts, which calls for what most educators would consider significant changes to standard practices. Effective close reading instruction relies on a thorough understanding of the non-negotiable aspects that support this rigor.

2.  **Be clear about guidelines.** Most state education departments provide flexible guidelines to districts regarding the use of specific standards-based methods and materials for close reading instruction. Even though you may be required to follow specific instructional guidelines, you often will have some flexibility based on your expertise as a classroom professional. It is important to understand and monitor how much leeway you have so you know your options.

3.  **Don't assume that using packaged materials or district-provided materials will ensure effective close reading instruction.** Delivering close reading instruction relies on the quality of your professional knowledge, judgment, and decision making. Packaged and district-provided materials can support your efforts, but your ability to monitor and adjust your instruction based on careful assessment of your students is critical.

4.  **Use close reading to address the needs of struggling learners and English Language Learners.** Close reading requires students to use grade-level materials, but it does not exclude the use of scaffolds for struggling learners. Many standards ask students to master rigorous skills, but they also encourage the use of supports to assist learners who are reading below grade level.

5.  **Stay open-minded and adopt a can-do attitude.** Close reading is hard at first, and it can also be difficult to make the necessary changes in mind-set. For all the reasons we think we can't possibly succeed, surely we can!

## Professional Development Activities

- Survey your knowledge and experience with the non-negotiable characteristics of rigorous reading on page 8. You may wish to share your views and practices with colleagues and note questions or concerns that you will seek guidance on as you continue working through the book.

- Determine how closely your experiences align with the pertinent practices described on page 9. Place a check alongside those practices that align well with your current classroom activities and a star alongside those that you wish to revisit.

- Review the teacher-friendly definition of close reading on page 7. Consider ways you might adjust or refine this definition so that it becomes your own.

# Chapter 2

## Lesson Design and Delivery

Let's begin by considering how close reading lessons fit into a larger literacy framework. Close reading is one component among many that aids literacy development. Even though it is a very significant component and may routinely require 30–45 minutes of instructional time, students and teachers still do many traditional activities including those listed in the chart below.

| Students | Teachers |
|---|---|
| • Read independently<br>• Practice other literacy routines (e.g., building vocabulary through word work, improving fluency, strengthening spelling, journaling, and more)<br>• Participate in literacy activities with peers<br>• Self-select texts for independent reading | • Support students' independent reading<br>• Read aloud to students<br>• Provide guided reading instruction and practice<br>• Differentiate small-group instruction<br>• Encourage students' peer-led literacy activities (e.g., literature circles)<br>• Monitor and adjust instruction as needed<br>• Create an environment that supports literacy growth and development |

Integrating close reading into your classroom will not replace these other components, but it will require you to make some significant and thoughtful adjustments to your mix of instruction and the amount of time you spend on each activity. For example, you might consider ways to flexibly rotate activities. Additionally, your mix of activities may change from year to year depending on the needs of your students. Still, because close reading is a significant way to support reading development and is standards-aligned instruction, it will likely become the focal part of your instruction around which the other activities take shape.

Although our emphasis is on close reading, we continue to provide small-group guided reading instruction and consider it of primary importance. We weave the two methods together into a flexible approach based on the Hourglass Language Instruction Model described on the next page. To help our most struggling readers better meet grade-level reading expectations, we need to build their foundational skills using leveled materials or support them in other ways as needed. Likewise, our proficient and advanced readers also benefit by extending their skills.

# The Hourglass Language Instruction Model

The Hourglass Language Instruction Model (Soto-Hinman & Hertzel, 2009) aims to fill literacy gaps for English Language Learners and Standard English Learners. The process calls for students to move from large heterogeneous groups with broad instruction to intensive, homogeneous groups of students with similar proficiency in language skills.

In our use of the hourglass model, students first participate in whole-class, grade-level close reading instruction. Afterward, they gather in small guided-reading groups for basic skill instruction, and then return to a whole-class setting where the lesson is concluded. We employ a common theme in order to link the instruction and unite content and skill.

We initially adapted this model specifically to address the needs of our struggling learners. We were very concerned about this group, who seemed neglected amid the sweeping national reform. What we came to understand was that the hourglass model presents the perfect venue for close reading, enabling us to weave our analytical instruction together with our basic skill instruction in a way that makes sense for *all* our students.

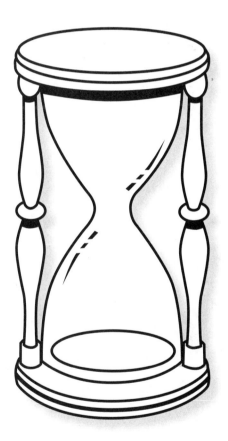

**Whole-class, grade-level close reading instruction**
(analytical, deep reading and complex texts)

| **Small-Group Instruction Group 1** | **Small-Group Instruction Group 2** | **Small-Group Instruction Group 3** |

**Differentiated instruction** provided in basic reading skills as an intervention (using leveled materials) or an adaptation (assisting with grade-level materials)

**Whole-class, grade-level close reading instruction**
(analytical, deep reading and complex texts)

# Whole-Class Close Reading Instructional Routine

A close reading lesson involves the following steps, which you can easily adapt to reflect your personal teaching style:

## Close Reading Process

**Step 1**
- **Day 1:** Teacher introduces text briefly, providing little, if any, instructional guidance.

**Step 2**
- Students read text independently and interact according to instructions.

**Step 3**
- Teacher reads text segment (500 words) aloud while students follow along.

**Step 4**
- Teacher asks guiding questions and assigns tasks, while students participate in discussion/tasks.

**Step 5**
- **Day 2:** Teacher recaps and begins process for new text segment.

**Step 6**
- **Day 3:** Teacher recaps and begins process for new text segment and concludes with activity.

Other typical design and delivery features of a close reading lesson include:

Text passages are often short yet very rich and worthwhile (roughly 1,500 words total).
Daily reading is roughly 500 words.
Length of instruction is typically 30–45 minutes several times a week (with additional small-group skill instruction).
An entire passage together with questions, tasks, and academic discussions is completed in 3–7 days.
A culminating activity typically concludes the instruction.

The circle graph at the right shows a rough approximation of the time commitment for each part of the instructional sequence.

## Time Allotted for Close Reading Routines

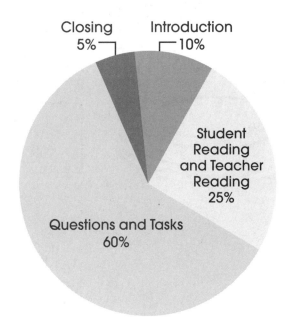

Closing 5%
Introduction 10%
Student Reading and Teacher Reading 25%
Questions and Tasks 60%

*Close Reading for the Whole Class* • © 2015 by Sandra K. Athans & Denise Ashe Devine • Scholastic Teaching Resources

This instructional approach is very different from the approach we use in other types of reading activities, including small-group, guided-reading instruction and even read-alouds. The emphasis here is on working through and analyzing the text closely, carefully, and cohesively. The emphasis is on rereading, thinking through and discussing critical ideas, breaking down the text structure, looking closely at word choice, delving into the intent of the author, and determining the overall cohesiveness of student ideas, views, and understanding. Although this may still sound as if it parallels what you already do, the most significant difference is that little time is spent *outside of the text*. In other words, very little time, if any, is spent on pre-reading activities. You will not typically preview or pre-teach vocabulary. Also, you will spend very little time introducing the topic, tapping students' background knowledge, or urging students to make connections. Additionally, during close reading, conversations about the text will not often stray from explicit or inferential evidence found in the text. When personal opinion, personal connections and experiences, and an unsupported train of thought enter the discussion, you need to quickly yet carefully divert the conversation back to the text.

## Critical Reading Strategies

As you begin to grasp the more distinctive design and delivery elements of close reading instruction, it will come as no surprise that your students will also need some distinctive new reading strategies, which we define here as new behaviors and supports. We have found that the following five strategies suit close reading well and help students succeed with this challenging style of reading:

1. **Launching Jump-Start Clues:** Students independently perform a quick visual inventory of a passage, glean information about it, and make flexible, knowledge-based assumptions about content, genre, and more. This is a student-initiated, pre-reading scaffold.

2. **Text-Marking:** In this method of coding a text, students mark specific areas of the text or note ideas in the margins. Text-marking codes are mostly drawn from skills within the standards. (Students use sticky notes when the material cannot be marked directly.)

3. **Listening to My Inner Voice:** Students rely on this internal meaning-making mechanism when noting ideas, asking questions, and describing feelings. Other triggers of engagement are carefully tracked and monitored and shown in their text marking.

4. **Pursuing Evidence:** Students sift through passages, hunting for and prioritizing evidence and ensuring that their assumptions and inferences square with the actual text. They show this skill in their text marking and class discussions.

5. **Allowing the Passage to Speak for Itself:** Students analyze a passage deeply, identifying its unique content, structure, and purpose. They demonstrate this ability in text marking, class discussions, and through formal or informal assessment.

We've introduced these strategies here because they are inseparable from close reading, and the design and delivery of close reading instruction relies on their use. A deeper discussion on these strategies appears in Chapter 8.

# A Glimpse Inside a Real Classroom

Now that we've explored the structure and aims of close reading instruction, let's observe the type of dialogue you might hear on Day 1 of a close reading lesson early in the school year. Students have had basic instruction in the reading strategies at this point and are now applying what they know as they tackle a new passage. The introduction, middle, and closing of a lesson are featured.

## Lesson Introduction

Students sit at desks clustered into groups of four to five students each. The teacher has distributed a packet of materials to each student containing a multiple-page reading passage and questions and tasks.

| Teacher's Words | Teacher's Observations and Actions |
|---|---|
| *Today we are going to begin reading a passage I think you're really going to enjoy. The section we'll be reading today begins on the first page and extends onto page 2. Would everyone turn to page 2 and look midway down the page for the word "Stop"? This marks the end of the section we'll be reading today. Let's turn back to the first page.* | Teacher observes that all students are clear about the directions and offers no further introduction to the text. |
| *Remember, you're going to be "reading with your pencil" and marking your thoughts as you construct meaning. You can circle unknown or interesting words, underline critical or emphasized ideas, and note sentences or sections that are unclear with a question mark.* | Teacher observes all students are on page 1 and picking up their pencils for text marking. |
| *If you finish, you can reread the section and begin writing gist statements or make one or two careful observations about the author's writing style. Are there any questions so far?* | Teacher pauses briefly to answer students' questions. |
| *Before you begin reading, would you launch your jump-start clues and construct a working idea of the genre and content of this passage? Please do that now and note your idea on the first page. As you know, you can change your mind after you read. Please complete that shortly and then begin your reading.* | Teacher observes students as they skim and scan the passage and note genre/content ideas on the front cover. She then observes students' reading behaviors as they read and mark the passage. |

This sample lesson features a selection of the reading strategies discussed earlier. Launching jump-start clues, text marking, and listening to their inner voice are skills students can begin to practice early in their close reading activities. The other strategies—pursuing evidence and allowing the passage to speak for itself—will be applied later in this lesson.

## Close Reading: A Progressive Approach

From this brief sample, it is clear that there is another significant matter affecting the delivery and design of close reading lessons—the progression of the approach. Providing an understanding of and a plan for sequencing your close reading instruction is what our Megaphone Approach, shown below, is all about. This approach amplifies the idea that close reading skills develop gradually and build over time with repeated practice. It also highlights students' progress as they begin to master complex analytical skills. These are approximations, and you can pace the transitions according to the individual needs of your students.

**Megaphone Approach to Close Reading**

**Beginning lessons** are delivered at the beginning of the school year.
**Students learn and practice how to:**

- Read without teacher scaffolds
- Apply jump-start clues (with mini-lessons)
- Reread to reexamine meaning and to consider other elements of the text (e.g. author style, word choice)
- Recognize and listen to inner voice
- Use methods of text marking (to align CCSS skills in Key Ideas and Details, Craft and Structure, Integration of Ideas within grade-level standards)
- Identify and use evidence
- Participate in class discussions
- Answer text-dependent questions
- Complete text-dependent tasks

**Intermediate lessons** are delivered when students make adequate progress, usually by mid-year.
**Students learn and practice how to:**

- Apply jump-start clues to a variety of genres and gain accuracy in reshaping ideas while reading
- Reread to reexamine selected areas in a text or the entire passage to take in other elements of the text
- Gain confidence listening to inner voice (with practiced skills) and rely on an inner voice to build new skills
- Gain efficiency in text marking (with practiced skills) and extend its use to build new skills
- Gain efficiency in locating and using evidence
- Gain skill with discussions
- Gain skill in answering text-dependent questions
- Gain skill in completing text-dependent tasks

**Advanced lessons** are delivered when students make adequate progress, usually by the end of the school year.
**Students practice or master how to:**

- Apply the jump-start process to unusual and challenging passages and gain accuracy and speed in shaping and reshaping ideas while reading
- Reexamine text passages based on their needs
- Trust a "knowledgeable" inner voice
- Apply strategic text marking
- Wield evidence to support views
- Contribute to and benefit from classroom discussions effectively and efficiently
- Respond to text-dependent questions concisely
- Complete text-dependent tasks effectively

## The Middle of a Lesson

The teacher monitors students' independent reading and circulates around the room, observing their text-marking activities, level of focus and attentiveness, and timing. The teacher also takes a mental inventory of who completes the reading and, when most students are finished, prepares to read the passage aloud.

| Teacher-Student Dialogue | Teacher's Observations and Actions |
| --- | --- |
| **Teacher:** *I realize that some of you may not have finished your reading and that's okay. I've also noticed that some of you completed it and returned to the passage to reread or to note new observations. I'm now going to read the passage aloud and I'd like you to follow along with your pencil. Look for your question marks and see if my reading might help clear up some of your misunderstandings.* | Teacher observes that all students are clear about the directions and then reads the passage. |
| *I'd like you to take a minute or two and share your text marking with an elbow partner. Explain your thinking, share areas that might have confused you, and also share any new insights you may have gained based on reviewing the passage during the teacher read.* | Teacher listens in on student conversations, determining if any patterns emerge that may need addressing. She also gauges students' level of understanding of the passage. |
| *First, I'm pleased that you're gaining skill with identifying the genre of the passage when you launch your jump-start clues. Would someone from Table Group A share their experience with the jump-start clues?* | Teacher begins classroom discussion of jump-start clues. Since students are reasonably successful with this (confirmed earlier in the lesson), she moves through this quickly. |
| **Aiden:** *Kareem and I thought this was realistic fiction so we began to look for the problem.* | |
| **Teacher:** *Great. Thanks, Aiden. Would someone from Table Group B like to add to Aiden's response?* | Teacher selects students from different table groups. |
| **Cadence:** *Alexis and I thought it was realistic fiction, too. We knew that the main character was the girl, Bev, and that the story was from her point of view. But she doesn't tell us everything.* | |
| **Teacher:** *That's an interesting observation. So although the story is told from Bev's point of view, as readers, we still don't know exactly what she's thinking all the time. This is sometimes called limited point of view.* | Teacher highlights key ideas in student's response to help build knowledge, such as that point of view can be "limited." |

| Teacher-Student Dialogue | Teacher's Observations and Actions |
|---|---|
| *Alexis: Yeah, we both underlined and starred the sentence where Bev walked away from the coach. Even though she didn't say what happened, we knew she was disappointed about something because of her actions.* | Teacher listens attentively to the discussion, knowing that some of the text-dependent questions address this tricky part of the passage. |
| *Cadence: And it was a little confusing because she made the soccer team. And we both thought she would be happy about that. So even though we were a little confused, we knew that the problem in the story was starting to develop.* | |
| *Teacher: So you believe she should have been happy to make the team, yet she wasn't. As readers, we don't know why Bev was disappointed, but we aren't meant to know this. Hmmm . . . I wonder whether the author is trying to confuse us. I see that many of you share Cadence's uncertainty about Bev's reaction. The passage does get mildly tricky. Let's move forward and tackle some of the questions on page 3 and dig a little deeper.* | Teacher lingers on this point because she intends to discuss the author's intentions, an aspect of reading that many of her students struggle to grasp. |
| *Would someone from Table Group C read the first correlated question aloud? Let's be sure we understand what it's asking, and then I'll give you some time to locate your evidence and share your thoughts with your group.* | Teacher moves through the questions and tasks. |

In the middle part of the close reading lesson, the teacher does the following:

Monitors student progress and steps in to provide assistance as needed. Are students confused by the sight of text when it is formatted in columns? Do they return to read captions or are they skipping the visuals altogether? Are they reading too quickly? The monitoring guidelines on the next page list a number of signals to look for as you monitor students' independent reading and text marking. Some teachers like students to share their ideas in group brainstorming discussions before talking about the text in the whole-class academic discussion, so we've included signals for this.

Evaluates students' level of engagement with the passage and determines if supplemental instruction is required. You might choose to use teachable moments, offer mini-lessons, or add additional questions to help support student understanding.

Assesses how well students are incorporating previously taught reading strategies, including the jump-start clues, and determine if they need stronger support. Are students able to distinguish the genre when clues are present? If not, immediate action on your part is necessary.

Builds on student comments to reinforce skills or even to preview new skill areas you will introduce in subsequent lessons. This encourages students' participation and engagement, while demonstrating that there is an authentic purpose for learning new information.

Evaluates the lesson and its objectives, including the passage, questions, and tasks. Are things going as expected or are there surprises? Surveying the lesson—even in these early stages—is valuable and can help you make any necessary improvements.

## Monitoring Guidelines
### for Initial Stages of Close Reading Instruction,
### Independent Student Reading, Text Marking, and Sharing

**While independently reading, the student does the following:**

- Has eyes focused on text
- Is tracking with eyes, finger, pencil, and/or bookmark
- Demonstrates awareness of a sequence and a method of reading text, captions, columns, and so on
- Reads entire contents of a page, including captions, sidebars, callouts, and so on
- Has appropriate posture
- Shows signs of engagement (e.g., facial expressions, laughter)
- Demonstrates a reading rate seems appropriate (not too fast, not too slow)
- Demonstrates a slower pace and/or rereading in dense areas of text

**While text-marking, the student does the following:**

- Shows appropriate amount of text marking (not too much, not too little)
- Applies text-marking codes based on teacher instructions
- Makes text marks that fall within a range of accuracy based on teacher expectations
- Maintains a text-marking rate that seems appropriate and effective (not too fast, not too slow)

**While sharing ideas among table group members, the student engages in the following ways:**

- Responds when a classmate is speaking by making eye contact, acknowledging and responding to the speaker, and so on
- Shares text-based ideas connected to the question under discussion
- Actively works with classmates to clarify understanding of a question or the text

**To gauge the lesson's effectiveness, including the degree to which the passage draws in and engages students, the teacher might do the following:**

- Determine if students move through the text, adjusting their pace as you predicted
- Evaluate if students are detecting and marking critical points in the passage
- Monitor students' activity with content-rich, academic vocabulary
- Assess students' level of comprehension based on their initial comments with classmates
- Calculate the effectiveness of the questions posed and tasks assigned in guiding students
- Estimate students' level of struggle with the passage, questions, and tasks

The middle part of a lesson has distinct advantages for students, including the following:

**Repeated practice of beginning skills:** Students may need extra practice with unfamiliar skills. This might include simple skills like rereading, which for many students is a new phenomenon.

**Paired sharing:** Working with classmates before a group discussion can help build students' confidence and strengthen their collaborative skills.

**An acceptable balance of achievement and struggle:** Students improve on previously taught skills that they have practiced routinely, while also grappling with more complicated skills and reading material. This balance can provide the kind of encouragement that helps build stamina.

This part of the lesson typically takes the most time because deconstructing and analyzing a passage simply cannot be done quickly.

## Closing a Lesson

Although the closing only makes up about 5 percent of the lesson, each closing provides the opportunity to practice standards-based skills, such as summarizing, as well as new areas of emphasis in the standards that present challenges for students. For example, concluding with a discussion of the author's intentions encourages students to reflect on topics that may at first seem vague or uncertain. Also, you can identify where students are struggling and retrace the reasoning they used to help them make sense of difficult passages. Making this process as explicit and as transparent as possible helps students recognize and replicate it as needed. The end of a lesson is also a good time to gauge students' feelings about the process of close reading, collaborative discussion, and so on. Finally, your students' ability to identify the theme or main idea of the text segment lets you evaluate the success of your close reading lesson. The sample lesson shown below incorporates some of these techniques.

| Teacher-Student Dialogue | Teacher's Observations and Actions |
| --- | --- |
| *Teacher: You did a nice job reading this passage deeply. Let's sweep through a summary and review the important insights we uncovered during our close reading.* | Teacher builds students' summary skills through this oral review. She also recaps strategies students used to make meaning. |
| *In this fictional story, we meet the main character, Bev. We were immediately looking for the problem or conflict, since we know to expect this story element based on our knowledge of the genre, right? And what did we uncover, Jamal?* | Teacher highlights text structure and expectations to support jump-start strategy. She monitors students' reactions and engagement. |
| *Jamal: The problem was that Bev really didn't seem to want to play soccer even though she was really good at it. We didn't get this at first because she doesn't come right out and tell us her feelings. We all kind of expected that she'd really want to play since she was good at it.* | Teacher models attentive listening and nods as Jamal responds. |

| Teacher-Student Dialogue | Teacher's Observations and Actions |
|---|---|
| **Teacher:** *You're right, Jamal. We all agreed that the author made us work to figure out the problem. Question 2 uncovered how he did this, right? But <u>why</u> did he do this? Share a quick response with an elbow partner, then would someone from Table Group A like to share a response and show us how to think like the author?* | Teacher monitors students' reactions, references the response to Question 2, and poses a new question regarding author intention. |
| **Emily:** *He told the story from Bev's point of view, but he didn't let us know everything. He kept us searching and searching, trying to figure it out. We kept reading to find out what was up!* | Teacher nods in agreement and helps shape Emily's idea that students were "interested" in the story. She also uses the word "infer" to help Emily identify the strategy. Teacher moves discussion along. |
| **Teacher:** *Yes, we were really interested in the story and had to infer Bev's thoughts based on her actions. And there were some interesting twists and turns in the plot, right? I see a lot of you nodding, showing me you recognize the movement of the roller-coaster plot. Let's continue our summary and touch on these. Tyler, would you sweep through the critical events?* | |
| **Tyler:** *We originally thought she would be pretty bad at soccer. But then, she scored this incredible goal!* | |
| **Teacher:** *How did you know that it wasn't luck? Remember, we debated that a bit, right? Thumbs up if you remember that discussion. What evidence makes us absolutely certain that our understanding—that Bev was a skilled soccer player—squares with what the author intended? Who knows in Table Group B?* | Teacher recalls students' discussion where their ideas didn't square with the evidence in the story. She engages students with thumbs-up prompt and highlights the importance of returning to the text. |
| **Cadence:** *We went back to the story and found the author's use of words like "routinely," which we had to figure out meant that Bev always did well. And the author gave us other clues, too.* | |
| **Teacher:** *So we were fooled here and there and had to dig deeply here and there to gain meaning, sometimes by working through context clues to help us define unknown words we think were important. So how was the conflict resolved? We were all on the edge of our seats looking for the solution, but not having any idea what it would be, right? Maggie, please summarize the ending for us.* | Teacher monitors students' reaction and engagement and moves discussion along. She recaps the strategy of using context clues to figure out meaning of vocabulary. Teacher moves summary along. |

| Teacher-Student Dialogue | Teacher's Observations and Actions |
|---|---|
| *Maggie: We didn't know until the end that the coach was her dad, which was another twist in the plot, and that Bev played only to spend more time with him. But she got the nerve to tell him. He was surprised and they agreed to spend time doing other things together—and it was playing football!* | |
| *Teacher: How many of you feel you could write a summary of this? Now that we've reviewed the story, I'd like you to think a bit about the theme. I bet a lot of you already know the critical message the author shares in this story. Remember the theme is a big life lesson that isn't confined to the story. Take a couple of minutes to sketch out your ideas. Be sure to evaluate whether your idea is cohesive. Ask yourself: Is my idea emphasized from the start to the finish of the story? We'll review your good ideas tomorrow. Are there any questions about our reading or our discussions today?* | Teacher monitors students' response and feels confident enough that they are ready to move on to theme. She recaps basic ideas of theme to end lesson. |

Now that you are familiar with the design and delivery features of close reading, you can better imagine how it might fit into your classroom. To help you get started, we've included a sample mini-lesson for a first close reading lesson below. Questions and tasks for this mini-lesson appear on page 89.

# *Mini-Lesson:* Introducing Close Reading

This lesson is purposefully streamlined. Please adapt it to fit your passage. Also, interact with and monitor students in a manner that reflects your practices. Use your professional judgment when you model parts of the lesson, and make sure to utilize the technology you have available.

**Objective:** To introduce close reading          **Time:** 30–45 minutes

**Essential Question:** What is close reading, and how does it help us learn, develop, and strengthen our standards-based reading skills, which will serve us well now and in the future?

**Materials:** Close Reading anchor chart with definition (see page 7); a passage such as "The Champion of Quiet," and questions and tasks

**Guiding Questions:**
- What is close reading?
- Why is it used?
- How is it used?

*I'm sure many of you are familiar with close reading. You can use the anchor chart I've displayed as a reference. (Read anchor chart.) It's a method of reading we'll be using for part of our instruction. During close reading, we'll be reading shorter passages slowly, carefully, and more in-depth than before. Close reading passages often have rich and challenging content. They contain grade-level vocabulary words, sentence structures, and literary techniques. This makes the passages very interesting and engaging! Reading a short passage that is two or three pages long could take us several days. Rereading is also a part of close reading. With close reading, we gain a very valuable understanding of a passage.*

*Throughout the year, we'll be learning new strategies to help us with our close reading. Today, we're going to learn and practice our protocol, or the routine we'll follow for all of our close reading lessons. We're also going to work with evidence, or ways we can support our ideas about our reading by working through some questions and tasks. As you'll see, this is also a very important part of our close reading routine. The protocol we'll use goes like this:*

- *I'll hand out the passage, briefly introduce it, and then you'll read a section on your own quietly.*
- *After you finish, then I will read the section out loud as you follow along.*
- *Then we'll work together through questions and tasks.*

*(Distribute the passage.) I'm handing out our first passage. We'll be reading and digging deeply into this passage for several days. We'll be reading half of it today, half tomorrow, and then we'll wrap up our close reading activities on the third day. We'll be answering a few questions and completing one to two tasks each day.*

*Please write your name at the top of the page. If you scan down the passage, you'll see the word "STOP." That marks the end of the section we'll be reading today. If you finish reading early, please reread the section. It's really important that you not read on.*

*This first reading passage is called "The Champion of Quiet." I think you'll really enjoy it, and I selected it especially to start out the school year. I see everyone is set to begin, so I invite you to go ahead and read the first section quietly to yourself. (Monitor and mentally note students' reading behaviors. When nearly all students have finished, call an end to this independent reading time.)*

*Now I'm going to read the section out loud, and I'd like you to follow along in your text. (Read expressively and at a comfortable pace. Then hand out a sheet of questions and tasks to each student.)*

*This sheet contains the questions and tasks we'll be completing. There are three questions, marked "Q1" through "Q3," and two tasks. marked "Task 1" and "Task 2." Let's read the first question together.*

*Q1: What is Maggie's problem with Tuesdays? Use evidence from the passage.*

*Would everyone please underline the word "evidence" in the question and then think about what that word means? In about ten seconds, I'd like you to turn to your elbow partner and share your thoughts about the word. (Monitor students' discussions and continue with other observations.)*

*I heard a lot of very good ideas. I heard that evidence is "support" for your answers. I see you have a good understanding of what "evidence" means. Before we write our answer for Q1, we're going to go back into the passage and find and underline evidence for our ideas. After we underline our evidence, we're going to code it "Q1." Let's do that now. (Monitor students' underlining and mentally note their behavior. When nearly all students have finished, continue.)*

*I see all of you found evidence in the passage. Please take a moment to share your ideas with your elbow partner. Glance at your partner's passage and see where he or she has underlined evidence. Then, verbally share your response to the question. (Monitor and note students' interactions.)*

*I heard some very good responses. I also heard some good out-loud thinking as you shared with your partner. In particular, I heard some students clarify or make sure they found evidence that fully answered the question. For example, it's not enough to underline the second sentence in the passage and say that Maggie's problem was that she didn't like Tuesday's because of gym. That doesn't fully answer the question. Who can find additional evidence to answer this question more thoroughly? Would you point to the place in the passage where you think there is additional evidence . . . and if you haven't underlined and labeled this information, go ahead and do that now.* (Monitor and note whether students underline and label additional information.)

*How many of you have underlined evidence that Maggie's problem with Tuesday is that she has gym class AND she knows she will be picked last for a team? Also, this seems to happen every Tuesday. Although we don't know exactly how many times, we know it has happened often enough to make Maggie "hate" Tuesdays. Now that we've returned to the text and found evidence that helps shape a full answer to the question, let's pull these ideas together and write a response in the space provided on the sheet.* (Model writing a complete and thorough answer: "Maggie's problem with Tuesdays is that she has gym class and she knows she will be picked last for a team sport." This happens often, and she hates it. Move through Q2 and Q3 in this manner, making sure students have underlined evidence that aligns with the questions and are able to translate that evidence into a strong, cohesive answer.)

*Now that we've dug deeply and answered Q1 through Q3, let's take on a task. Sometimes you'll be completing the tasks on your own, but today we're going to do it together.* (Read aloud and then discuss how to approach Task 1.)

*Task 1: In your own words, explain what Maggie means when she says, "Maybe it was time for the Champion of Quiet to use her voice." Use evidence from the passage to support your answer.* (Key points: The text in quotation marks means the sentence is taken from the passage. Students should go back to the passage, locate the sentence, and underline it. Next, they should reread it in context and then begin to shape ideas for completing the task. They will likely need to pull evidence from several areas in the passage and paraphrase the evidence into a cohesive answer. Finally, they should use the insights they've gained working through Q1 through Q3 to help answer the task. Model this response so students have an understanding of expectations. You can also use this as a model for similar tasks students will encounter in other close reading lessons.)

*Now that we've dug deeply and responded to Task 1, let's tackle Task 2, which is a different kind of task.* (Read and discuss how to approach Task 2.)

*Task 2: Use the space below to make a list of synonyms and antonyms for the word "blue."* (Key points: Task 2 is a different kind of task. It supports students' word-building and figurative-language skills and is critical to their understanding of the passage. As before, students should go back and reread in context all uses of the word "blue," which should already be underlined from working through Q1 through Q3 and Task 1.)

*That's it for today's lesson. I trust you have a better understanding of close reading. I also notice you're beginning to understand what evidence is and how to use it. On a scale of one to five fingers, how many of you feel you have a really strong understanding? I also think you're really enjoying the story about Maggie and her dilemma at school. Tomorrow, we'll finish our reading.* (Pool your observations about students' performance and rank your concerns to help determine students who will need small-group support instruction.)

## The Flexibility of Close Reading

Classroom configurations vary greatly depending on student abilities, and school professionals have to make adjustments based on what they believe will best aid their students' achievement. Additional concerns, from scheduling and length of instructional reading time to class size, make each classroom a unique learning environment and discourage a cookie-cutter approach to close reading.

To begin, we've provided a snapshot of three different classrooms to demonstrate the flexible manner in which close reading can be adjusted to suit the diverse needs of teachers and students alike.

✰ **Classroom A:** In this inclusive sixth-grade classroom, students receive their main instruction from their teacher with support from an instructional specialist, who closely monitors four students who have a history of difficulty with reading comprehension and have been identified as high need.

This classroom uses instructional reading material provided by the school district that includes a selection of complex text passages and suggested lessons/activities. The material aligns well with the curriculum and offers opportunities for a variety of whole-group and small-group instruction. To supplement these program lessons, the teacher carefully selects close reading passages. He wants to enhance his students' comprehension by using texts that align with specific social studies and science curricula. He also looks for passages that will give his students practice in the literary skills that he identified as being underrepresented in the program lessons. For these supplemental texts, he has created questions and tasks that guide students through the passages and also targets their needs.

While the class moves back and forth between the required and supplemental material, the teacher skillfully monitors and adjusts his instruction based on observations of his students' performance. Often, the instructional specialist will offer additional feedback or examples for her students. In some instances, she will scribe their discussions and then help students use the written notes to pull ideas for their written responses to questions or tasks.

Since students master the nuances of close reading strategies and recording responses at different rates, the amount of support may vary within the class. The goal is for all students to complete their close reading with high comprehension and independence.

✰ **Classroom B:** Classroom B is a third-grade, small-group instructional intervention class with one reading specialist and six high-need students who are currently reading at least one full year below grade level. Many of these students have limited background knowledge of the content of the passage.

The reading specialist is working with the same on-grade-level complex text passages as the grade-level classroom teachers, yet she has enlarged the passage and copied each paragraph on a separate page. Early in the school year, the reading specialist often models text-marking strategies (in a similar manner to how the classroom teacher presents them) or the small group works together to mark only one passage.

Several months into the school year, students have mastered and refined several of the reading strategies to help themselves work through the paragraphs more independently. Some students move to corners of the room where they can read and reread out loud. Others read one line at a time, tracking with a small pointer. Students underline, highlight, write main ideas in the margin, and monitor their understanding. They come together in groups after reading and marking each paragraph to compare notes. They discuss challenging words and compare how they figured out their meanings. They discuss main ideas and author's purpose. The reading specialist facilitates discussion and allows students to debate and correct one another in a respectful and supportive manner. The consistent and comfortable setting allows students to safely share their thoughts and understanding, as well as the chance to refine and change their thinking as they converse with their peers.

This classroom is paced slower than that of their on-grade level peers. Yet, these students can usually grasp the big idea of the complex, context-rich text they read.

✰ **Classroom C:** This is a fourth-grade class with a fully integrated language arts and social studies curriculum. The classroom consists of regular education, special education, and non-special education students identified as at risk. A special education teacher and reading specialist provide some in-class and pull-out instruction.

In the fall the class is working on a unit called "Our Big World," which focuses on the Haudenosaunee Confederacy (called the Iroquois Confederacy by the French). Much of the reading material (small-format informational text and complex articles) comes from the state education department's website. Supplemental materials compiled by the teacher parallel instruction with the state's suggested lessons. The lessons on the Haudenosaunee provide a range of detailed nonfiction reading material and focus on text features and incorporate writing instruction. The supplemental materials both support the unit and expand instruction to include topics including oral tradition, legends, cultures that help shape our community, and early government.

The teachers are providing vital reading, writing, and content-area instruction simultaneously. As the teachers detect gaps in their students' understanding, they insert abbreviated, close reading lessons with carefully selected text to help students comprehend the content. They use a variety of reading passages, supplementary text, and websites along with questions and tasks crafted to foster deeper understanding.

This class may spend several days on a small-format informational text such as *The Iroquois League* (Randolph, 2003) and then move on to an article about the Iroquois Constitution, followed by a multi-day lesson on folktales. Over time, teachers will circle back to the original text and help students understand the connections among these topics.

It's evident from these classroom snapshots that there are many ways to integrate close reading instruction into your classroom and to work with standards-aligned materials so you can best address your students' needs.

## Scheduling Close Reading Instruction

Shown below are a variety of classroom schedules showing flexible ways to fit close reading instruction into your classroom.

- **Close reading as the main focus of ELA instruction time**
  *Approximately 30–45 minutes per day for 3–5-day clusters*
  For 3–5 days the majority of ELA instructional time is devoted to close reading activities. The class works through an entire passage, participates in class discussions, and completes aligned tasks. Following this period, the class moves on to strategy instruction, literature circles, genre studies, author studies, mini-lessons, guided reading, or another type of reading instruction. After this, the process repeats with a different close reading passage for 3–5 days.

- **Close reading as a daily portion of ELA instruction time**
  *Approximately 15–30 minutes daily*
  A portion of every ELA block is dedicated to close reading. Students read a passage independently or with a partner and review questions on one day. On the next day, they underline evidence or write evidence-based responses. On the third day, students share their responses and participate in a class discussion. The remaining ELA time each day may be spent on other types of reading instruction as described in the first schedule.

- **Close reading rotating schedule**
  *Entire ELA time is used for close reading for 1 to 2 weeks*
  The class focuses on skills related to tackling complex texts, text marking, identifying evidence, contributing to focused class discussions, and writing evidence-based responses. One lengthy passage or several theme-related passages may be used throughout this period. Afterward, the class may take a brief break for a mini-lesson, strategy instruction, reading a novel, or other type of ELA instruction. Within a week or two, the class begins another close reading unit.

■ **Close reading with full-length texts**

*Flexible*

While the class is using a full-length text for reading instruction, a portion of the text can be used for close reading instruction. Some chapters can be used for more traditional reading instruction, including the reader-response approach. Alternating chapters, or even excerpts, should be carefully selected for a more thorough analysis using the close reading approach. This format is ideal for teachers who desire or are required to use several lengthy novels as a part of their instructional program.

■ **Close reading during other class time**

*Flexible*

Close reading instruction does not always happen during reading class. Teachers are often able to incorporate close reading instruction into their writing block. Likewise, when the passages are selected to align with content curricula, content-area instructional time can be used for close reading instruction.

## Forming Small Groups for Guided-Reading Instruction

As you saw in the Hourglass Language Instruction Model on page 13, students also meet in small groups for guided-reading instruction in addition to whole-class close reading. You can form these small groups according to your students' needs. For instance, struggling readers may meet with the teacher for 20–30 additional minutes, while average and skilled readers may meet for 15–25 additional minutes.

## *Five Tips* for Lesson Design and Delivery

1. **Monitor your pacing and don't be too hard on yourself.** Allow yourself some miscalculations. Even veteran teachers have to wrestle with challenges that crop up in the course of a lesson. Sometimes lessons will have to move forward even if some students haven't completed every aspect of it. Spending too much time on any one task can quickly diminish student enthusiasm and motivation. Discreetly acknowledge students who are unable to finish activities and encourage them to finish during small-group reading, if needed. Additionally, some lessons may take a bit more time than you have planned. Determine how you might accommodate such a change and select the option that has the least impact on your schedule.

2. **Avoid rigid, over-planned close reading lessons**. We are not encouraging you to take a haphazard approach to lesson design and delivery, but sometimes over-planning can cause you to miss your students' compelling insights, views, or ideas. Be prepared for such surprises and use them wisely.

3. **Build your students' independence and then protect it.** Once you begin providing close reading instruction, your students will quickly grasp the routines. They will also begin to assume responsibility for their own learning. For example, they will apply jump-start clues and text marking; they will regulate their reading rates based on the complexity of texts; they will check their own understanding against text evidence and author intentions; and they will recognize that productive struggle is okay. Encourage your students to continue moving forward with this independence by protecting it. In other words, don't do for them what they can do for themselves.

4. **Stay focused on the lesson objectives.** It's easy to get sidetracked. Monitoring your focus and your students' focus is important and can be trickier than you might imagine. There are several reasons to stick to the lesson objective. First, there is a lot of ground that must be covered. Rich texts can be

analyzed from many different angles, and helping students through the ones you feel are most critical takes time—which you must guard. Also, you must monitor students' level of engagement through all stages of the design and delivery process. There is a point of diminishing returns. The transition to reading shorter passages more deeply often presents challenges for some students.

5. **Some students rely too heavily on others.** Each student must participate and contribute. If some students rely too much on others, discuss this issue with them individually and come up with a plan for making adjustments. Boost students' self-reliance by letting them know that you will call on them at specific times. This way they can be prepared and consider what they will say. You might also encourage students to change partners or participation groups, which often increases on-task behaviors.

## Professional Development Activities

- Review the steps of the close reading process described on page 14, as well as the lesson examples on pages 19–23. Discuss your feelings about the lesson process with colleagues. Determine ways to adapt the process to better suit the needs of your students, as well as your schedule.

- Examine the classroom snapshots on pages 26 and 27. Also review the close reading scheduling suggestions on pages 27 and 28. Consider ways you might integrate close reading into your classroom. Share your ideas with colleagues.

- Review the mini-lesson on introducing close reading that begins on page 23. Discuss ways to adapt this to use in your classroom with your colleagues. What would you like to modify? Are there areas that you expect to be challenging to students? Consider how you would adjust the basic lesson to address their needs.

# Chapter 3

## Text Selection

The major changes in standards and curriculum present us with a major challenge: *How do we find appropriately challenging, meaningful texts that also keep students engaged and motivated?*

## Setting Steep Expectations

Demanding that our text passages meet our steep expectations is not at all unreasonable. In fact, it would be unreasonable *not* to demand this. Done properly, close reading requires a lot of time and energy. The best way to make this investment pay off is by ensuring that the passages you choose are deserving of your students' attention. Your scrutiny, even of district-required materials and other preassembled or packaged selections, matters greatly.

**Note:** Throughout this chapter, we refer to reading materials using a variety of terms, including *texts, passages, text selections, works,* and *books.* The terms we use and the strategies we present apply to all of the forms you will likely use in your close reading instruction: stories, articles, poems, speeches, excerpts from books and historical documents, and more.

### Changes Promoted by Standards

The Common Core State Standards and most other standards call for a rigorous learning environment that encourages high-level student thinking and participation, including the following:

- Students must read a balance of informational and literary texts and gain content-area knowledge through reading those texts.
- Students' reading skills must keep pace with grade-level expectations.
- Students must be able to provide text-based answers, cite evidence in their writing, and build a strong academic vocabulary.

If these changes leave you wondering if your current materials can help you meet these new challenges, the answer is *maybe*. Even as many of us are in the midst of transitioning our text materials by making adjustments independently, adopting district-required materials, or adapting materials from reputable sources, you will want to gauge and monitor your use of materials carefully. Let's begin by addressing one of the greatest hurdles facing teachers today: the balance between teaching literature and informational text.

## Literature Versus Informational Text

The call to balance our use of text types caused concern among many elementary classroom teachers, including us. We feared our beloved narratives were swiftly becoming an endangered species—and facing possible extinction! How could we let this happen, when narrative stories are often a child's earliest exposure to text? Might we be robbing students of valuable learning during those early elementary years? Narratives present the perfect springboard to launch numerous lifelong reading lessons. Our initial fears have faded as we've come to understand that narrative texts remain a vital part of the elementary school curriculum. That being said, we'll briefly explore the kinds of changes that do affect our text selections.

★ **50/50 Balance:** As outlined in the National Assessment of Educational Progress (NAEP) guidelines and reflected in the CCSS readiness objectives, elementary students should be completing one-half of their literacy instruction with literature, primarily fictional texts, and one-half with informational texts. One way to view this change is through the chart below, which shows the CCSS recommendations about text types for grades K–12. As you can see, stories are still well represented in grades 2–6. We have also found that fulfilling the informational half of our instruction has made our curriculum stronger—a very significant revelation!

## Text Types Grades K-12

| LITERATURE | | | INFORMATIONAL |
| --- | --- | --- | --- |
| Stories include: | Dramas include: | Poetry includes: | Literary Nonfiction; Historical, Scientific, and Technical Texts include: |
| **Grades K–5** | | | |
| children's adventure stories, folktales, legends, fables, fantasy, realistic fiction, myths | staged dialogue; brief, familiar scenes | nursery rhymes; narrative poems, limericks, free verse poems | biographies, autobiographies; books about history, social studies, the arts; technical texts: directions, forms and information displayed in graphs, charts, maps; digital sources on a range of topics |
| **Grades 6–12** | | | |
| adventure stories, historical fiction, mysteries, myths, science fiction, realistic fiction, allegories, parodies, satire, graphic novels | one-act and multi-act plays in written form and on film | narrative poems, lyrical poems, free verse poems, sonnets, odes, ballads, epics | exposition, argument, and functional text in form of personal essays, speeches, opinion pieces, essays about art or literature, biographies, memoirs, journalism; historical, scientific, technical, or economic accounts (including digital sources) for a broad audience |

☆ **Knowing Where Our Students Are Heading:** Content-area classes now include informational texts covering history/social studies, science, and technical subjects—beyond those considered within language arts instruction. Following the direction these avenues lead to, it comes as no surprise that at grades 8 and 12, the use of informational over literary texts is recommended. Keeping watch over where our students are going better equips us to grasp our role in helping them get there.

## Text-Selection Strategies to Enrich Your Existing Resources

Being mindful (and accepting) of the need to carefully balance materials and gauging the degree to which our current materials were doing this was a critical step for us. We created the text-selection strategies described below to help us through this ongoing process. A sample of a partially completed recording chart for each strategy appears below.

☆ **Informational X-Ray:** Sometimes a fictional story contains important information. For example, many of our fourth-grade classes read *Samuel's Choice* by Richard Berleth, a work of historical fiction that nevertheless can be put under the microscope for close reading. Taking an "informational X-ray" of some of your current texts can help you locate sections that incorporate historical information within the larger narrative. It is critical, however, that you verify the facts in historical fiction. Authors often take creative liberties, so you might have to consult author's notes, footnotes, and so on, for information on how fact and fiction have been blended in the text.

### Informational X-Ray

Title/Author: <u>Samuel's Choice</u> by Richard Berleth

| Page # | Fact-Based Information to Highlight |
|--------|-------------------------------------|
| p. 6 | use of mills to grind wheat into flour using water power and grinding stones |
| p. 12 | role of the Sons of Liberty in the Revolutionary War and their posting of Declaration of Independence |
| p. 14 | arrival of General George Washington in New York and the regional battles there |

☆ **Informational Spark:** While looking at your current reading material with these new 50/50 expectations, you may also find that some of your literature has enough of an "informational spark" to assist you in reaching your goals. For example, a third-grade unit on tall tales could be supplemented with informational texts on historical travel along the Mississippi River, the westward movement, and the business of logging. Locating these kinds of brief supplemental passages in your school library is a quick way to support your instruction while balancing the type of texts or text passages you use. Likewise, many content-area resources and textbooks are rich with nonfiction and informational passages.

Selecting an informational passage from a social studies text about the Erie Canal, for example, would nicely supplement the reading of *The Eerie Canal* (Reber, 1998), a time-travel adventure story geared for grades 3–6.

## Informational Spark

Title/Author: Mike Fink, Paul Bunyan, and other Steven Kellogg selections
(Literature Unit: Tall Tales)

Title: Mike Fink

| Page # & Spark | Supplemental Topic to Highlight With Informational Text |
| --- | --- |
| Author's Note | pioneer travel and transportation/westward expansion /topographical geography of U.S. |
| p. 2–end | biographical account of Mike Fink: recounted in Henry Howe's *Historical Collections of Ohio* and Miami Valley Historical Society *Miami Valley Vignettes* by George C. Crout |
| p. 30–32 | arrival of steamboat transportation |

Title: Paul Bunyan

| Page # & Spark | Supplemental Topic to Highlight With Informational Text |
| --- | --- |
| p. 3 | the business of logging |

⭐ **Pairing Texts:** A final activity to explore is pairing your favorite texts. For example, Grace Lin's well-loved *Where the Mountain Meets the Moon* (2009) could be paired with *Dragons and Serpents* (McCall & Regan, 2011), an informational text on these mythological characters. Locating a "just-right companion" to your beloved favorite may seem like a daunting and time-consuming task, but the knowledge you gain from reexamining your classroom favorite during your informational x-ray or informational sparks review will aid you immeasurably in this task. Inspiration might strike as you peruse new books purchased by your school media specialist at the start of the school year, while browsing the shelves of your local bookstore, or though reaching out to colleagues in other districts with good ideas to share. As mentioned earlier, this mindful gauging is an ongoing process that becomes routine.

## Paired Selections

Title/Author: <u>Where the Mountain Meets the Moon</u> by Grace Lin

| Companion Nonfiction Text<br><u>Dragons and Serpents</u> by Gerrie McCall<br>and Lisa Regan | Relationship<br>Both feature dragons; both are linked<br>to Chinese culture. |
|---|---|

Title/Author: <u>Because of Winn-Dixie</u> by Kate DiCamillo

| Companion Nonfiction Text<br><u>Rescue Dogs</u><br>by Kristen Rajczak | Relationship<br>Both feature strong relationships between<br>owners and dogs; both showcase animal<br>intelligence and helpfulness. |
|---|---|

Title/Author: <u>Roll of Thunder, Hear My Cry</u> by Mildred D. Taylor

| Companion Nonfiction Text<br><u>The Montgomery Bus Boycott</u> by Kerri O'Hern<br>and Frank Walsh | Relationship<br>Both portray issues of racial inequality<br>and struggle. |
|---|---|

## Text Selection Strategies for New Materials

In addition to inventorying and supplementing your existing nonfiction materials, you may still need to locate other resources. In so doing, consider the following parameters:

☆ **Evaluating Text Complexity:** Text complexity matters greatly, and considering grade-level complexity is also a significant departure from the differentiated and leveled reading approach many of us practiced earlier. The criteria in the Common Core Model of Text Complexity model on the next page is one indicator that will help you evaluate potential new text selections and retire those that no longer fit in your overcrowded curriculum.

It is vital that you consider all three components in this model when selecting new texts, whether or not you are using packaged materials provided by your district. As classroom teachers, your professional judgment and ability to validate the complexity level of a text is unmatched.

The **Quantitative** measure calculates the difficulty of a text by considering measures such as word count, word length, frequency, syllable count, sentence length, and other factors. These measures are often computer generated or determined with well-known readability levels such as Lexile, Guided Reading Level (GRL) or Degrees of Reading Power (DRP). Although a quantitative measure is valuable, it cannot be the sole guideline for choosing texts for your students. Some texts express complex ideas through simple language. John Steinbeck's *The Grapes of Wrath* (1939), for example, which falls at a 2nd-grade Lexile level due to its simple language, is actually more appropriate for high school and college students.

# Common Core Model of Text Complexity

**QUANTITATIVE**
word length, word frequency,
sentence length,
text cohesion
(Computer Generated)

**READER AND TASK CONSIDERATIONS**
Reader: motivation,
knowledge, and experience
Task: purpose, complexity,
and types of questions posed
(Professional Judgement)

**QUALITATIVE**
meaning or purpose,
structure, language
conventionality, and clarity
that knowledge demands
(Professional Judgement)

Adapted from Appendix A of the CCSS for Literacy and English Language Arts

### TEXT COMPLEXITY GRADE BANDS AND LEXILE RANGES

| CCSS Text Complexity Grade Band | Former Lexile Ranges | Lexile Ranges Aligned to CCR Expectations |
| --- | --- | --- |
| K–1 | N/A | N/A |
| 2–3 | 450–725 | 450–790 |
| 4–5 | 645–845 | 770–980 |
| 6–8 | 860–1010 | 955–1155 |
| 9–10 | 960–1115 | 1080–1305 |
| 11–CCR | 1070–1220 | 1215–1355 |

Source: www.corestandards.org, Appendix A, p. 6

The **Qualitative** measure of text complexity requires teachers to use their professional judgment. You will want to consider students' previous exposure to the content and genre. Will they have enough background knowledge to untangle the meaning or purpose underlying a complex piece of writing? Some amount of struggle is acceptable, even helpful, but where do you draw the line? The structure of a particular text and its language conventions are other areas you'll want to consider. New subject matter, a novel theme, or an abstract idea may be very challenging for some students, even if the reading ability required to comprehend it is low.

The **Reader and Task Considerations** measure claims that much of a text's readability depends on the reader, the task, and the relationship between the two. We have all had students who have chosen to read a book beyond their reading level, yet were able to tackle it with success due to their high interest in its content or previous experience with it. Knowing what may be of major interest to one student and a stumbling block to another is vital to your ability to choose appropriate reading material.

☆ **Special Accommodations:** English Language Learners and students with disabilities may need accommodations or extra support in one or more of these areas. Keep in mind the goal of avoiding a knowledge gap if at all possible.

## Evaluating the Standards for Specific Features

In addition to reviewing the text complexity criteria, don't forget to take a close look at the applicable standards from your state. The chart below contains literary must-haves according to the CCSS College and Career Readiness Anchor Standards for Reading. For example, CCSS Grade 3 Reading Literature Standard 3 states that students should be able to "describe characters in a story and explain how their actions contribute to the sequence of events." As such, you would look for stories or dramas that feature well-developed, rounded characters whose actions clearly contribute to the plot as it unfolds. Other must-haves together with the anchor standard they address are featured in the chart below.

| LITERATURE | Key Ideas and Details | Craft and Structure | Integration of Knowledge |
|---|---|---|---|
| Stories<br>Drama<br>Poetry | • Strong characterization and story elements (3)<br>• Valuable theme or central message (2)<br>• Inferencing (starting at grade 4) (1)<br>• Key details and examples (1) | • Thoughtful word choice (4)<br>• Writing techniques including alliteration and many others depending on genre (5)<br>• Figurative language (5)<br>• Varying text structures (4-6)<br>• Text cohesion (5)<br>• Character viewpoint (6)<br>• Challenging point of view and author background (6) | • Varied visuals/ graphics (illustrations and artwork) (7)<br>• Literature that can be compared with other forms of media (7)<br>• Literature that can be compared to similar works or other works by the same author (9) |
| **INFORMATIONAL** | | | |
| Literary Nonfiction<br>Historical Texts<br>Scientific Texts<br>Technical Texts | • Key details: 5 Ws (1)<br>• Inferencing (starting at grade 4) (1)<br>• Main idea(s) (2)<br>• Relationship between historical concepts, ideas, or technical elements (3) | • Domain-specific vocabulary (4)<br>• Variety of text structures: comparison, cause/effect, problem/solution (5)<br>• Variety of text features that encourage efficient informational intake (5)<br>• Author point of view (6)<br>• Multiple accounts of same event (6) | • Varied visuals/graphics (charts, graphs, diagrams) (7)<br>• Text that can be connected to multi-media resources (7)<br>• Author provides multiple means of valid evidence. (8)<br>• Text that can be compared or integrated with other texts on the same topic (9) |

# Strategies for Locating Materials

A variety of sources that can help you balance your text types so that your passages align with complex text standards and meet grade-level Lexile levels are described below.

✭ **State Education Departments:** Many state education departments have excellent resource materials that are available for free on their websites. You may find that your state is perfectly aligned and that other states have useful information in different formats. If your state does not have a site, you might wish to explore those of other states.

✭ **School Library:** One of the first places we checked when looking to update our instructional material was our school library. Although we found some books that met our needs, we focused on finding periodicals, such as *Highlights, AppleSeed,* and *National Geographic Kids.* We pulled dozens of articles that matched the themes outlined for our grade level. Next we evaluated each article for length, variety of sentence structures, vocabulary, structure and characteristics, overall content, and other elements to determine if it had the necessary rigor. Sometimes our selections reflected our own judgment (see the 5S Teacher Read on page 40). At other times we relied on online sources, such as the Lexile sites listed below, to guide our decision making. Our school media specialist steered us toward nonfiction books that were appropriate for elementary readers, as well as an exchange program for borrowing books from other libraries.

✭ **Internet Sites:** Sites such as readworks.org, grolier.com, and a-zbooks.net, bookwhere.net, newsbank. com, and teachingbooks.net were valuable resources in our quest to find complex reading materials, as well as desired topics, levels, and genres. We learned that our school district subscribed to some online resources with up-to-date materials that aligned with the Common Core Learning Standards (CCLS). Many free websites, such as newsela.com, lexile.com., Scholastic Book Wizard (www.scholastic.com/bookwizard) and Scholastic Lexile Levels Made Easy (www.scholastic.com/parents/resources/article/book-selection-tips/lexile-levels-made-easy), allow you to adjust the Lexile level of a passage or find similar passages at a range of reading levels. We stumbled onto several sites that had outdated or less desirable tools, which underscores the importance of being critical and using careful judgment in your text selection.

✭ **Student Newspapers and Magazines:** There are many student news magazines and newspapers that feature articles on current world news events and hot topics. These periodic publications often include data, charts, graphs, maps, and photographs. If a topic covered in one of these publications matches a curricular objective exceptionally well, we reserve these copies to use in the future rather than allowing students to take them home. The teacher guides that may accompany these magazines often list additional resources and websites on the topic.

✭ **Public Domain and Fair Use Materials:** Websites that provide free access to writing and literature in the public domain are also good places to look for complex texts. These repositories offer works published prior to 1923 whose copyright has expired. Classic works of literature make good sources that can be used, adapted, and excerpted in close reading. Project Gutenberg (https://www.gutenberg.org) is a quick-access site with excellent materials. In addition to printed materials, public domain audiobooks are available at no charge at sites such as LibriVox (librivox.org). These can be helpful for addressing standards that ask students to work with content presented in diverse media and formats.

✭ **Resources From Professional Reading, Social Studies, and Science Organizations and Events:** We attended local and national reading conferences, where we were able to collect updated bibliographies and lists of soon-to-be-released titles that aligned with the CCLS. These conferences also provided us with an opportunity to network and collaborate with other educators seeking to meet the goals of close reading. If you are unable to attend conferences, you might peruse the professional publications that your district subscribes to.

⭐ **Award-Winning Books:** We were surprised to learn how well the many different categories of book awards align with new areas of emphasis in the CCSS and other standards. For example, the annual Robert F. Sibert Informational Book Award goes to the author of the most distinguished informational book published in English during the preceding year. The 2012 winner, *Balloons Over Broadway: The True Story of the Puppeteer of Macy's Parade* (Sweet, 2011), continues to be a favorite in our classrooms. Here is a list of other awards.

- Outstanding Science Trade Books (www.nsta.org/publications/ostb)
- Notable Social Science Trade Books for Young People (www.socialstudies.org/notable)
- Jane Addams Children's Book Awards
  (http://www.janeaddamspeace.org/jacba)
- Giverny Award for author and illustrator of best children's science picture book (4–8)
  (http://www.15degreelab.com/givernyawardwinnerlist.html)
- Schneider Family Book Awards (www.ala.org/awardsgrants/schneider-family-book-award)
- Astrid Lindgren Memorial Award (www.alma.se)
- Hans Christian Andersen Award (www.ibby.org)
- The United States Board on Books for Young People (www.usbby.org/awardslists.html)
- New York State Reading Association Charlotte Award

⭐ **Book-Length Works:** Although shorter passages are used for close reading, book-length works are suitable, too. Many state education department websites include recommended book-length works for close reading. Use an excerpt of the text that can support an in-depth, analytical close read or plan a combination of approaches, such as independent student reading or teacher read-aloud and close reading to move through the entire text in a timely manner. Sample assignments for a fourth-grade lesson, along with CCSS correlations, based on an excerpt from *Where the Mountain Meets the Moon* (Lin, 2009) appear on page 42. The same holds true for informational text such as documents, speeches, and letters.

⭐ **Multicultural Texts, and Historical, Scientific, and Technical Texts Resources:** Multicultural texts mirror global views and concerns and can often spark students' interest and increase their participation. Selecting informed and culturally responsive texts is therefore critical. Many authorities recommend careful review of cultural works, especially retellings, for example, questioning how close a retelling is to the authentic versions and comparing literary elements including plot, theme, setting, characterization, point of view, and style. In addition to consulting your school media specialist or public librarian, investigate the following resources:

- "50 Multicultural Books Every Child Should Read" [University of Madison, available through the National Education Association (www.nea.org)]
- "How to Choose the Best Multicultural Books"
  (www.scholastic.com/teachers/article/how-to-choose-best-multicultural-books)
- Children's Literature Resources (www.ctreading.org)
- Children's Literature Association (www.childlitassn.org)
- Multicultural Books for Younger Children (www.bankstreet.edu)
- Multicultural book awards dedicated to children's and youth literature
  (libguides.nl.edu/content.php?pid=20655&sid=145694)

■ Sources for literary criticism:
*Kirkus Reviews* (www.kirkusreviews.com)   *School Library Journal* (www.slj.com)
*Horn Book* (www.hbook.com)

This kind of investigation will also serve you well as you select informational texts. An awareness of multiple perspectives and points of view is critical in the context of historical events and ideas. For example, selecting a passage that includes the British perspective on the Revolutionary War is an effective way to enrich students' understanding of this event.

## Text Selection Strategies That Support Professional Development

It takes intelligence to recognize what we don't know. While revisiting the non-negotiables on page 8, you may stumble upon one or two content topics that are mildly unfamiliar. It's possible that some of the new content areas emphasized in your standards reach beyond your comfort level and shake your confidence for a number of different reasons: you question your level of knowledge on the new topic, you're unsure how to address new topics that may be sensitive, you may not be confident that your ability to provide an analytical level of instruction in the new areas is up to par, and/or you lack experience with the kind of structural analysis specified in the standards.

✫ **Consider the Source of Your Material:** If you are unfamiliar with some topics or suspect that they might contain sensitive issues, be sure to select materials from credible sources. We've already discussed using caution in selecting Internet sites, but even more due diligence may be required here. Scrutinize the source just as you would scrutinize the material. Is the source reliable, responsible, and current?

In addition to your own research, seek reliable assistance. This could mean asking your literacy specialist for help. It could also mean that you take extra precautions with special kinds of materials, such as multicultural, historical, and scientific texts.

✫ **Strengthen Your Knowledge of Unfamiliar Topics:** It's important to familiarize yourself with some of the lesser-known topics that might tie in to your close reading. These might range from mythology to classic poetry, from text structures to poetic technique. Identifying your needs and taking action to strengthen your knowledge is critical. Just as the standards have created changes in our classrooms, so, too, have they added opportunities for new avenues of professional development.

Today, professional development takes many forms. Professional Learning Communities are professional teacher-led inquiry groups, in which participants determine a topic of study, organize an agenda, and establish meeting times. Many states education departments support these groups and offer small grants to participants who fulfill their obligations. Collaborating with others in a professional book club is another way to build your knowledge. Committing some time to sharing feedback on potential resources is also helpful as you make your way through the research that will point you toward the right materials. Taking courses, conducting independent research, and participating in online activities are additional avenues to explore.

## Text Selection Strategies That Address Student Motivation

Thus far, we've presented text-selection strategies that address the standards and the shifts that have come with them. There are also practical matters to consider while making your text selection, tried-and-tested techniques that extend beyond the standards and into the mechanics of today's classrooms.

✩ **Bring on the Engagement:** Your materials should be of genuine interest to your students. This is particularly true for close reading, as students will be reading the same passage multiple times. If there's nothing to get them interested in the first place, it's highly unlikely that their third reading will improve the situation. Selecting passages that are current, relevant, and feature high-interest topics is more important than ever!

✩ **Create an Engaging Context:** It's not easy to get students to a level of genuine enthusiasm for a particular text. Be prepared to create a stirring context. For example, while working with classic speeches or excerpts from historical documents, sharing some insights about people, places, and events can help boost student interest. Even though you don't offer pre-reading support during close reading, you can still seek to spark student interest. This can be done through text-dependent questions and performance tasks.

✩ **Uncover and Discover:** Most students will not reread a passage—no matter how short it is—if they don't recognize the benefits of doing so. When selecting passages, be sure the content is sufficiently engaging to attract and hold your students' attention. If not, some students won't give it a second chance.

✩ **Accept Academic Struggle:** Don't exclude a passage because there are dense areas where you know students will encounter difficulty. This view is very different from our instruction with leveled and differentiated reading materials, yet this technique encourages perseverance, guides students in a new direction, and often reinforces learning.

## Putting It All Together: The 5S Teacher Read

We designed the five steps in the 5S Teacher Read to serve as guidelines to direct your text-selection process.

✩ **Step 1: Skim and Scan:** Take a quick visual inventory of the text. There may be unusual features, such as pictures, fonts, and spacing, that present good opportunities to trigger a "reader alert" that will guide students to notice unusual features of the text. Quickly examine titles, subtitles, callouts, and other content-related features that can give you clues about the genre.

✩ **Step 2: Scour:** Read a passage and break it down into sections. On a typical day, we read from 500–750 words, but we are flexible. If a passage has an especially dense section, if the author has used a complex literary technique, such as allusion or allegory, or if there are other reasons to slow down your average close reading pace, make this adjustment. Flag areas of struggle (AOS), which could be vocabulary, dense text, figurative language, complex ideas, unusual features, quirky styles, blended genres, and so on.

✩ **Step 3: Savor:** Next, take a closer look at the meaning of the passage, including themes or critical ideas. Gauge the level of evidence the author has provided to support these deeper-level concepts, and review this evidence in the context of the author's intentions. This is a demanding step but it's a valuable one; if the passage doesn't hold up under your scrutiny, opt to exclude it from a close reading unit.

✩ **Step 4: Start Over:** Once you've determined that the passage holds up, read it again to make sure you can validate your ideas about the passage from start to finish. This stage lets you check the cohesiveness of your ideas.

⭐ **Step 5: Survey Results:** Continuously monitor your selection process based on practical classroom experience. As you get to know how your students work with a passage, make any necessary adjustments in your lesson plans or in the manner in which you provide close reading instruction in certain areas. Recognizing the importance of this ongoing follow-through is critical.

In conjunction with the 5S Teacher Read, use a Close Reading Checklist. Samples of a 5S Teacher Read and a Close Reading Checklist for "The Champion of Quiet" appear on pages 43–45. Although we no longer use this checklist, we still work in two-person teams to discuss our ideas about a passage.

# *Five Tips* for Text Selection

1. **Take a long, hard look at favorite texts.** Acknowledge the spirit of your standards while using the strategies in this chapter to help with text selection. For example, if you continue to use your fiction favorites, doggedly pursue ways to balance your instruction with worthwhile and substantial nonfiction. Determine if some of your texts no longer fall within the complexity band for your grade level and replace them.

2. **Challenge but trust your professional instincts.** As you seek out and review new texts, you'll question whether your students will be able to read them. You'll also gauge your comfort in teaching new topics, and how much time you can commit to them. Challenge yourself to try new materials, yet also be prepared to adapt them so they work for your classroom. Case in point: We adopt texts provided by our state education department, with two provisions. First, we only use a selection of the available materials, and second, we make our selections carefully.

3. **Supplement district-assigned or packaged materials.** You might find that some of the materials you must use fall short in a given area—interest, suitability, currentness, and so on. Use the strategies in this chapter to find materials to fill these gaps. As you'll recall from Chapter 1, close reading is a component of a much larger literacy approach. See if you can use your science, social studies, art, and other curricular areas to introduce supplementary texts.

4. **Don't despair because of lack of funds.** Many of the strategies we suggest do not require you to have an extensive budget for new materials. Acknowledge that the text-selection process is not something that can change overnight, and recognize that it is not a static process. Prioritize your text needs (such as by reviewing new areas of emphasis in the standards) and address them as your budget allows.

5. **Don't underestimate your students—and prove it!** Your students need to know that you believe in them and their abilities. Using phrases such as, "I believe you can do this" and "I know your efforts will be worthwhile" help convey this important message to our students.

## Professional Development Activities

▪ Go on a Text-Selection Scavenger Hunt. Using any of the text selection strategies in this chapter, (1) devise a plan for supplementing an existing resource; (2) locate a new literature passage; (3) locate a new text passage for classic literature; (4) locate a historical informational passage; and (5) locate a text passage on a lesser-known topic. Share your experiences with colleagues.

▪ Using any of the passages you selected for the first activity, perform the 5S Teacher Read process on it with your colleagues. Discuss the outcome and also reflect on your use of the 5S Teacher Read and how you might adjust the process to make it your own.

▪ Review the five tips above. Share your experience and more helpful advice with colleagues.

# Close Read Assignments for
## *Where the Mountain Meets the Moon*
### by Grace Lin

Chapter assignments are listed in the chart below. For some assignments, you will complete Close Reading Activities. (Close Reading Activity A is shown below.) For the other assignments, you will choose one of the Engaged Reader Response Activities shown below.

| | |
|---|---|
| Chapters 1–5 Close Reading Activity A | Chapters 26–30 Engaged Reader Response |
| Chapters 6–10 Engaged Reader Response | Chapters 31–35 Engaged Reader Response |
| Chapters 11–15 Engaged Reader Response | Chapters 36–40 Engaged Reader Response |
| Chapters 16–20 Engaged Reader Response | Chapters 41–45 Engaged Reader Response |
| Chapters 21–25 Close Reading Activity B | Chapters 45–End Close Reading Activity C |

✭ **Close Reading Activity A:** Reread the following passage from pages 1–2 and answer the questions below.

"Far away from here, following the Jade River, there was once a black mountain that cut into the sky like a jagged piece of rough metal. <u>The villagers called it Fruitless Mountain because nothing grew on it and birds and animals did not rest there.</u>

Crowded in the corner of where Fruitless Mountain and the Jade River met was a village that was a shade of faded brown. This was because the land around the village was hard and poor. To coax rice out of the stubborn land, the fields had to be flooded with water. <u>Villagers had to tramp in the mud, bending and stooping and planting day after day. Working in the mud so much made it spread everywhere and the hot sun dried it onto their clothes and hair and homes. Over time, everything in the village had become the dull color of dried mud.</u>"

1. The underlined sentences best support the idea that the villagers (RL.4.1)
    **a.** are unhappy yet accepting of their lives  **b.** hope to change their working conditions  **c.** feel crowded
2. What is the importance of these paragraphs? (RL.4.3)
    **a.** They introduce the characters and suggest the problem in the story.
    **b.** They describe the dreary setting and suggest the problem in the story.
    **c.** They inform readers how to grow rice by flooding land with water.
3. What is the meaning of the word *coax*? (RL.4.4)
    **a.** to cut back on  **b.** to grow with difficulty  **c.** to coach or instruct

**Engaged Reader Response Activities:** Select two to three activities and record your responses in a reading journal, discuss your ideas with a classmate, or share your ideas in a reading group.
- Summarize key events that take place in these chapters. (RL.4.2)
- Describe in depth a character, setting, or event using specific details within these chapters. (RL.4.2)
- Record five new or interesting words (with definitions) in these chapters and explain how you determined their meaning based on context clues. (RL.4. 4)
- Describe how the illustrations or other visual features in the story contribute to what is conveyed by the words. (RL.4.7)

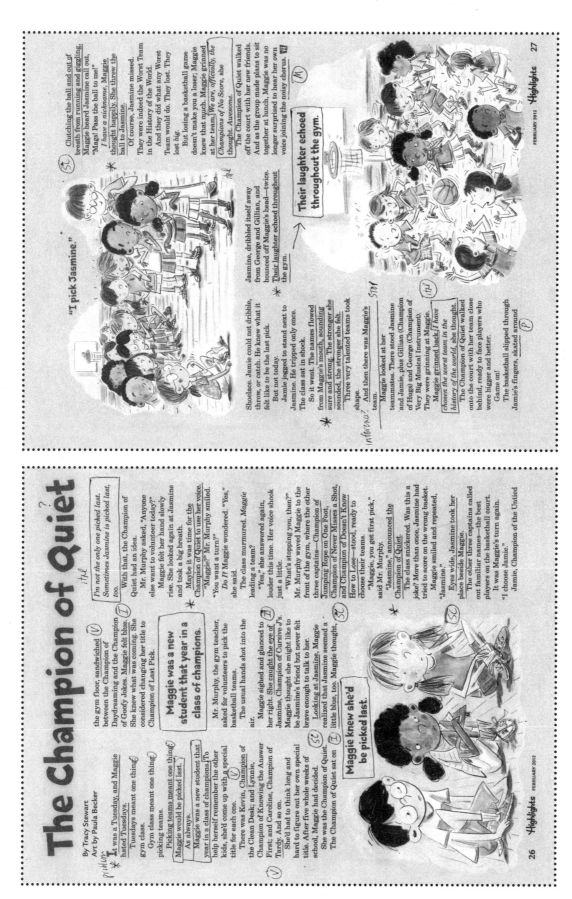

These are the markings we made on our own first pass of "The Champion of Quiet."

# A Master Teacher's 5S Process for "The Champion of Quiet"

## STEP 1: Skim and Scan

My quick visual inventory reveals these features:

- illustrations of children (some unhappy)
- three-column text
- callouts
- indented text, dialogue—looks student friendly
- ironic title?

There is enough here to suggest genre: fiction or realistic fiction. Title and illustration may hint at conflict.

## STEP 2: Scour

Story is about 750 words. Areas of Struggle (AOS):

*Vocabulary:*
- champion (unfamiliar)
- tardy (new)
- sandwiched (used as verb)

*Figurative Language:*
- Personification: "basketball skated" "noisy chorus"
- Metaphor: "Maggie felt blue,"
- Idioms: "caught the eye of"

*Punctuation:*
- use of repeated colon at beginning
- use of long dash throughout

*Features:*
- callouts
- italics for character's thoughts

*Sentence Structure (tricky):*
- introductory and parenthetic clauses in beginning and middle of sentences

*Other:*
- Inferences: "And then there was Maggie's team."
  Areas of struggle are moderate. I'll break into two sections for close reading.

## STEP 3: Savor

I'll slowly review story to identify and examine themes and critical ideas, then decide which ideas are best emphasized by text evidence.

Maggie, the main character, accepts her inability to play basketball but becomes a good friend to others. She dares to change the gloomy routine of her Tuesdays. She steps outside of her comfort zone and unites a team of similar basketball underachievers in friendship. In the end, Maggie receives a nickname from her new friends.

Acceptance of self and others is a strong theme; ample evidence supports this theme.

Theme is a common one, but story contains unique and unexpected events. *Examples:* Maggie's team is terrible and still loses, but prize is new friendships. Maggie's skill in empathizing with others and trying to change the situation is also unique. These twists will pose good challenges for students. *Themes:* acceptance of self and others, empathy, courage, independence, self-reliance, and capability

Maggie was a new student, yet she initiated change, rallied others, and improved an unpleasant situation for new friends and herself.

## STEP 4: Start Over

I'll review the story to make sure my ideas about the themes are cohesive throughout the story. I'll use story elements to loosely guide me.

*Problem:* Maggie's Tuesdays are dreadful, which is compounded by other troubles—she's a new student, she's shy, and she doesn't have any friends. *Solution:* Solution occurs when Maggie determines, "it was time for the Champion of Quiet to use her voice." The pivotal event occurs when Maggie volunteers to be team captain. *Events:* Maggie boldly selects Jasmine first—a classmate she'd like as a friend. Even Jasmine is "wide-eyed" over this unexpected event. Maggie then continues to select a group of other underachievers and feels "strong" about her selections. The team is a disaster on court, but their laughter "echoed throughout the gym." Also, Maggie is given a real nickname—Mags—by Jasmine. Their concerns are not on playing well . . . and are certainly not on winning. In the end, the awesome "Champions of No Score" make plans to sit together at lunch. Maggie has overcome her troubles and helped others as well.

My ideas square with the story; there is ample evidence to support them.

## STEP 5: Survey the Results

Step 5 will take place following the delivery of my lesson, but I must plan how to observe it so I can make adjustments as needed.

- Take notes to determine how well students approach the story during close reading. I'll note their success with jump-start clues (including genre and detection of other features that help them launch their own pre-reading efforts).
- Determine how students progress through the AOSs identified earlier. I'll note areas I might want to omit and/or others I might add to my list for the following year.
- Gauge my pacing; Monitor students' analysis of theme(s) and determine their success with identifying and using evidence.

*Close Reading for the Whole Class* • © 2015 by Sandra K. Athans & Denise Ashe Devine • Scholastic Teaching Resources

# --- Close Reading Text Checklist ---

**Title** "The Champion of Quiet"          **Author** Tracy Stewart

**Source** HIGHLIGHTS Magazine          **Length** 750 words

1. **Literature** or **Informational** (circle one); **Genre:** realistic fiction

Comments: good exemplary passage for realistic fiction; contains typical elements, such as
illustrations, and problem/solution structure poses a just-right amount of challenge for students

2. **Text Complexity Measures:**

A. **Quantitative   Lexile Level:** 500          Below Range      Within Range      Above Range

(word/sentence length, syllable count)      **(X)**              (   )                 (   )

Comments:   below range for fourth grade but a good passage to start with in fall; will help
students transition back to school by enabling them to review some skills and strengthen others;
also well-suited as an introduction to close reading for reasons below

B. **Qualitative Measures**              Low            Moderate         High

(e.g., student exposure, text structure,    Complexity      Complexity      Complexity

language conventions, knowledge          (   )            **(X)**          (   )

demands, and so on)

Comments:   Students must use inferencing and other complex skills likely to be challenging, such
as recognizing literary techniques including idioms and grasping complex sentence structures. They
must also evaluate the meaning of varied features such as italicized text.

C. **Reader and Task Considerations**        Low            Moderate         High

(e.g., motivation, engagement, attitude)     Appeal         Appeal          Appeal

                                          (   )            (   )          **(X)**

Comments:   Students will enjoy the plight of the main character, who steps out of her comfort
zone in order to unite a team of challenged, yet good-humored basketball players. The story
highlights acceptance and true friendship—themes that are authentic, motivating, and familiar.

3. **Standards Alignment and 5S Teacher Read Analysis**

A. Key Ideas and Details  Passage is helpful for building students' inferential skills. Questions and
discussion should target key ideas and details that will guide students to examine Maggie's motives
and feelings that are not stated. Title can help direct students to overall theme, which is familiar but
presented in a unique way through a nickname.

B. Craft and Structure  Figurative phrases, complex sentence structures, text features, and
interesting uses of punctuation can be explored. They work together to support the author's
intention. Readers will need to investigate these (e.g., the use of italics to show a character's
thoughts) to correctly interpret events.

C. Integration of Knowledge  Passage serves as a good anchor text for students throughout the year.

# Chapter 4

## Text-Dependent Questions

Since close reading aims to help students gain and build knowledge, the questions we devise must support this objective. In part, text-dependent questions guide students through complex passages so they can gain new knowledge. Text-dependent questions are specific to the passage; they ask students to think through their reading analytically, and they should do the following:

- Rely on the text
- Align with the breadth of the standards
- Engage students
- Consider the author
- Withstand ongoing review

## Rely on the Text

Using text-based questions significantly changes the way we provide instruction. In the past, students were asked to call upon their background knowledge or move outside of text. Now, text-dependent questions ask students to base their responses solely on the text. The chart below shows non-examples and examples of text-dependent questions for "The Star Spangled Banner."

| Non-Examples | Examples |
|---|---|
| 1. What events led to the War of 1812? | 4. What is "the star spangled banner" referred to in the title? What evidence in the text supports your answer? |
| 2. Have you viewed a sports event where this song was sung? How did it make you feel? | 5. What is the meaning of the word *perilous*, and what context clues help you determine its meaning? |
| 3. Some people have criticized the ways in which performers have interpreted the lyrics to the national anthem at sports events. What are your views on the issue? | 6. Why do you think Francis Scott Key used question marks twice in the first stanza? Use evidence from the passage to support your answer. |

## Delving Deeper Into the Importance of Staying Close to the Text

It is important to stay focused on the text as you create questions, when you discuss and probe a passage with students, and as you define the parameters of acceptable responses to questions you intend to use for assessment.

For example, question 3 on the previous page might lead to an interesting classroom discussion, but if it moves the discussion too far from the text itself, this would be at the expense of helping students understand the meaning of the passage. Such questions have their value, and they may be useful to students during independent inquiry and research or as a component of a task.

Encouraging careful examination and reexamination of sections of a text is another reason to keep your questions closely related to the passage. Just as the self-questioning skills we used to teach our students are outdated by today's standards, the same is true of our previous experience with text evidence, also known as "supporting detail." Our text passages are more complex now. Passages that are rich in vocabulary and content make our search for evidence more challenging. In order to answer questions, students must often return to a section of a passage and read it multiple times. The idea that multiple readings uncover new evidence that builds understanding and supports success is at first a novel concept for students.

To determine that Francis Scott Key is referring to the United States flag as "the star spangled banner" in question 4 requires readers to glean evidence from multiple areas in the passage. What readers are being asked to see is that in "the dawn's early light" there are "broad stripes and bright stars" that are "streaming," which suggests that the "star spangled banner" is indeed the American flag. There is even reference to "our flag" in the sixth line. Gathering this evidence from the passage takes stamina and perseverance.

This type of repeated delving into the text helps students build their skills in identifying and using context clues to interpret the meaning of unfamiliar vocabulary words. For example, "The Star Spangled Banner" contains ample context clues to help students construct an approximate understanding of the word *perilous* referred to in question 5. Recognizing first that it is an adjective describing the word *fight* helps to place the word in context. Further descriptions of "rocket's red glare and bombs bursting in air" suggest the serious nature of the fight. Returning to the passage two to three times while applying these strategies (determining the part of speech and then corroborating with synonyms or synonymic phrases) to make meaning takes the kind of reading stamina that close reading supports and builds—provided that students are encouraged to use these strategies inside the text.

Close reading instruction consciously excludes supported and unsupported opinion, personal connections, guesses, inexact recollections, and vague paraphrasing. Your instruction and questions should steer students away from generalizing or personalizing in these ways. Questions 1–3 exemplify this kind of meandering away from the essence of a text. Even though the War of 1812 has a connection to the passage, question 1 is not answerable based on information provided in the text. Likewise, question 2 is a personal connection question and could steer instruction away from the passage. Question 3 is a matter of opinion. Again, there is value to these types of questions. But during close reading, questions should lead students back to the text, even though avoiding such questions can be tricky, and tugging students away from their personal views and connections can seem a bit harsh at times.

Inferencing is another skill that demands we regard the content of passages carefully. In order to make sense of complex text, students must read between the lines to fill in the gaps in ideas or events in a passage. Providing evidence for unspoken and sometimes scantily presented notions is a higher level of challenge that taxes students' skills. Even the terminology has changed; terms such as "nontrivial inferences," "logical inferences," and "evidence-based inferences" are used interchangeably within CCSS support material.

Inferences are not guesses or opinions. They are explanations based on evidence, and we can help our students make inferences through our text-based questions.

To answer question 6, students must make an inference as to why Francis Scott Key composed the first stanza using questions. Students could make a compelling argument that Key used these questions to express his profound disbelief that the flag had withstood the battle, supported by the text structure (the emphasis on using questions as a technique), and Key's vivid word choices.

As a result of the demands we see in today's standards, we can no longer instruct students to go back to the passage and pull out a few easy-to-locate details. Students often must excavate evidence from a passage through careful thought and analysis. They may need to back their claims with evidence that is unstated yet compelling, and they must also develop know-how in ranking the strength of this evidence. Helping students develop the skill, stamina, and savvy to do this is critical and can be achieved, in part, with carefully constructed text-based questions.

## Align With the Breadth of Standards

Keep in mind that your questions should not only align to your standards but also reflect their breadth, which is vast and far-reaching. For example, CCSS Reading Anchor Standard 5 calls upon students to "analyze the structure of texts, including how specific sentences, paragraphs, and larger portions of the text (e.g., a section, chapter, scene, or stanza) relate to each other and the whole." A question that analyzes text structure would align with this standard. Yet to cover the scope of the standard, students need to be able to analyze structure across a variety of genres, including informational texts, chapter books, dramatizations, and poetry.

Our practice today is to track the standards addressed by our questions and fill in the gaps as needed. We rely on our knowledge, expertise, and ongoing assessment of our students' performance to help guide our decision making about the types of questions we ask. We don't devote the same amount of time to each standard. Instead, we cover them based on our students' needs. For example, the non-negotiable characteristics of rigorous reading identified in Chapter 1 (page 8) address new areas of emphasis in the standards. We felt some of these areas, especially craft and structure, were more deserving of our instructional time than others. Because our students tend to struggle a bit with analyzing the relationship among sentences, scenes, and stanzas, we often include text structure questions to address this skill. Inferencing is another area that requires repeated practice, so we often include inferencing questions to improve students' proficiency. A list of questions we've correlated to CCSS reading standards appears on pages 55 and 56.

### The Passage Must Speak for Itself

Even though you should craft questions according to the content and scope of your standards, the content of each passage will determine how you do this. For instance, one passage might require a moderate amount of inferencing, so your questions would guide students to apply their inferencing skills. Another passage might require readers to grapple with multiple points of views, so your questions would target that standard. Similarly, a work of poetry would probably include questions about figurative language, while a passage describing a historic event would likely stress a standard that emphasizes organizational structure.

# Engage Students

Close reading works only when the passage is deserving of students' time and energy. The same is true for the questions you generate about that passage. Your questions must be alluring, inspiring your students to wonder in ways they hadn't before. As an example, consider the following two questions:

Question 1: *What is this passage mostly about?*

Question 2: *The purpose of a national anthem is to celebrate an idea or an event that is important to a nation of people. Using evidence from the passage, describe the event or idea that is celebrated in this stanza.*

The first question is generic and uninspiring. It may help determine whether students can analyze the content of a passage, but it may not motivate them to do so. The second question is grounded in the text itself. It has a context that adds interest and merit. It also supports students' understanding by offering useful information they may not have known.

Another point to keep in mind is that good questions can bolster and maintain a student's ongoing engagement if they are presented in a progression, where one leads to another, and another, and so on. Here is an example for "The Star Spangled Banner":

Question 1: *How much time transpires over the course of events described in this stanza? When does the event begin and when does the event end? Cite evidence to support your answer.* Possible answer: *The verse describes a battle beginning at "twilight" and continuing into the night. The verse ends as "dawn's light" approaches. The time that transpires over the course of the events is roughly a 12-hour period.*

Question 2. *Why is this element of the setting important? How does it engage the reader?*

Possible answer: *At night, there was tension over the events that unfolded unseen. Rockets glared and bombs burst. We sensed the uncertain outcome yet remained hopeful as each flash of light gave evidence that the flag remained standing. By the morning's light, the uncertainty ended. The battle was over, the flag remained standing, and our tension was replaced by relief and disbelief.*

These deeper, broader, and more probing questions should invite students to refine their answers, reshape their evidence, and reconsider their ideas and those of their classmates. As an example, you may get students in fifth or sixth grade to dig deeper into the stanza with a probing question such as this: *Identify the irony of the light cast by the rockets and bombs and explain how this contributes to the tone of the stanza.*

Some students will sense the irony that the rockets and bombs intended to destroy the land of the free and the home of the brave were sufficiently bright to reveal the "streaming" flag. These brief glimpses provided hope, reassurance, and comfort, and they add to the celebratory tone of the poem and its depiction of victory over adversity.

# Consider the Author

The role of the author is critical in close reading and is also highlighted in many standards. For example, CCSS Reading Anchor Standard 6 emphasizes the role of the author in text analysis, so some questions need to focus on the choices an author makes and on exploring the possible reasons behind those choices. Your questions can guide students to consider an author's decisions about the following elements:

- The use of a word or phrase
- The use of a particular text structure or feature
- The selection of examples and data to support an argument
- The omission of specific information

Here is an example:

Question 1: *Francis Scott Key uses some poetic techniques in this stanza. Identify one and describe how it contributes to the passage.* Possible answer: *The lines in the stanza follow a patterned-end rhyme: A, B, A, B, C, C, D, D. This rhyme creates a rhythm throughout the stanza, which unites the lines. The rhyme pattern also shows the careful thought Francis Scott Key gave to choosing his words; the meaning and the sound of the words both mattered greatly to him. Key not only tells an important story with words but also with memorable sounds.*

## Withstand Ongoing Review

As a final measure evaluating how well your questions meet your objectives, subject them to ongoing review. Carefully monitor your students' ability to answer them and share your results with colleagues who are using similar materials. You may find that, despite your conscientious efforts, you still need to adjust some questions to optimally support your close reading instruction.

## Crafting Questions

Although there are no ironclad rules for crafting good text-dependent questions, the diagram below presents a sequential action plan.

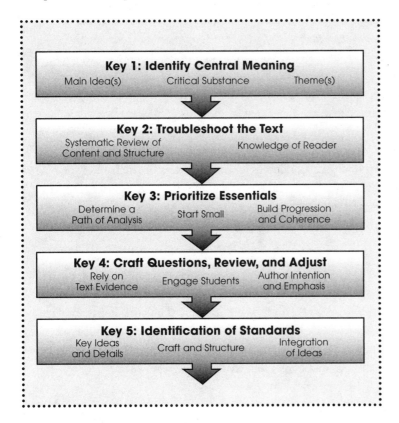

**The 5 Keys of Composing Text-Dependent Questions Action Plan**

⭐ **Key 1: Identify Central Meaning:** If you're working with a literature passage, determine its theme or themes. If you're working with an informational text, identify its main idea.

✰ **Key 2: Troubleshoot the Text:** Knowing the passage well is essential, so review it carefully prior to instruction. Your in-depth knowledge of the content and the structure of the passage helps you guide and support students' understanding through your questions. Knowing how your students will interact with the passage is also of great value. Anticipating where your students may struggle will help you scaffold their understanding with tailored text-based questions.

✰ **Key 3: Prioritize Essentials:** You will most likely need to prioritize the many areas of potential struggle you've identified in the passage and determine which ones will be most relevant to your students. Things to consider include which complex sections of text need to be broken up and which components of the text will deepen or expand students' comprehension skills. You may not be able to address everything you have flagged in your analysis, but prioritizing this way enables you to address some of these areas outside of your close reading instruction, such as during small-group instruction. You might also find opportunities to build them into a task, briefly slip them into your discussion, incorporate them into another facet of your close reading instruction such as students' text marking, or table them until you can reintroduce them in a subsequent mini-lesson.

Here are two tips that can help this process go smoothly: (1) It's important to start small. The benefit is that students' success with simpler questions may give them greater confidence when encountering the more complex questions that lie ahead. (2) Your questions should build progressively. After starting with vocabulary, they might jump to text structure and then to author intention. The important thing is to keep moving forward. Even if you are discussing a unique feature of the text, your focus should be on how the author uses that feature. It's important to provide context for your questions. Tackle complex passages head on, even if that means working piece by piece to get through them. The sample on page 57 shows this process for "The Champion of Quiet."

✰ **Key 4: Craft Questions, Review, and Adjust:** You've weighed and prioritized critical ideas, events, and areas of struggle. You've also planned your progression through the text. Now you're ready to craft your questions. Even though you have prepared rigorously, you will still want to review those questions and make any necessary adjustments. One good way to do this is by working with grade-level colleagues. Whether or not they have expertise in crafting text-based questions, their classroom know-how can be beneficial. The Case Study: Rigorous Review Using a Collaborative Approach on page 52 recounts our experience with this stage of the process.

✰ **Key 5: Identification of Standards:** To ensure that you're adequately covering all of the standards throughout the school year, make sure to note which standards you're covering in each passage. After progressing through The 5 Keys of Composing Text-Dependent Questions Action Plan, you will still want to evaluate your mix of questions and determine how the passage contributes to the scope of the standards.

## Using the 5S Teacher Read to Compose Text-Based Questions

The 5S Teacher Read, described on page 40, helps you determine if a passage will be a good match for your close reading instruction. As you'll recall, using this sequential process, you can determine if the ideas and themes in a passage are rich, relevant, and cohesive, as well as sift through the text for noteworthy vocabulary words, organizational structures, areas that rely on inferential thinking, and more. This analysis can help you craft effective text-based questions in the following ways:

In the **Savor** and **Start Over** steps, you determined themes or main ideas that held up under the scrutiny of multiple readings and in-depth review of the passage. This is Key 1 in the Action Plan for Composing Text-Based Questions.

In the **Skim and Scan** step, you identified instances that struck you as unfamiliar or unexpected, prompting you to wonder *What is this? Why is this here?* Text types such as how-to directions, sequential steps in a scientific experiment, assembly directions, and reviews of movies, apps, or software, often perplex students. Here are some questions that can help students identify tricky structures and gain comfort in analyzing less familiar types of passage formats:

- *Identify what type of text this passage is and explain its purpose. List two to three unique things you see in this passage that you would expect to find in similar passages.*
- *Why do you think the author presented this passage using this format?*
- *Why is this a good format for presenting the information? What advantages are there to the reader?*
- *How do the different structures used in this passage contribute to the overall meaning of the text?*
- *What key features distinguish the different structures from one another?*

Students will be using the jump-start strategy (introduced on page 15) to make some pre-reading inferences about genre and content. Acquainting them with these less familiar formats will enable them to develop this skill. Although these questions appear to stray from text evidence, they still serve the extremely useful purpose of helping students improve their skill at inferencing, which includes thinking flexibly.

Another helpful analysis is the **Scour** part of the process. This phase entails flagging areas of challenge, such as vocabulary, dense text, figurative language, complex ideas, unusual features, quirky styles, and blended genres. These areas comprise a treasure trove from which to create your text-dependent questions. Because you're covering a diverse variety of issues, you'll want to consider how to whittle them down efficiently. Use your areas of struggle (AOS) or your marked-up text as you tackle Key 3: Prioritize Essentials in the action plan.

# *Case Study:* Rigorous Review Using a Collaborative Approach

We first began creating text-based questions in teams of two or three. One reader would read aloud to the group in the manner of a classroom read-aloud—steady pace with expression, authentic pauses to read captions, view pictures, and so on. Our discussions centered on how to match our questions to the critical ideas we identified throughout the text, and then how to word the questions so they moved students' understanding toward the major themes or main idea of the text. Our discussions also addressed the range of plausible answers and the degree of flexibility we would allow when evaluating those answers for their use of text evidence.

These critical discussions helped us refine good questions into better, more effective questions. Below is a list of the kinds of questions we ask ourselves as we create text-dependent questions.

- *Do students need to read the text in order to answer the question? Must students return to the text to respond to the question?*
- *Does the question uncover an insight that is critical to the essence of the passage? Does it deserve student time and classroom time?*
- *Does the question guide students toward knowledge that helps them comprehend the greater meaning of the passage?*
- *Is there text evidence to support the question?*

- *Are there multiple pieces of evidence? What evidence best supports the response? Is the evidence located in the reading selection for that day?*
- *If the evidence is inferential, is it plausible based on what the author likely intended? What proof in the passage suggests the evidence aligns with the author's intentions?*
- *Have we considered the genre and the structure of the text and how these factors affect the content? Likewise, have we considered the author and how the craft behind the passage has steered the reader's understanding of it?*
- *What are some alternative views? Are they supported explicitly by the text? Are they partially supported with text evidence?*
- *Is this question appropriate during instruction or outside of instruction?*
- *Does this question contribute to the balance of questions in terms of difficulty, content, and standards covered?*

## *Five Tips* for Creating Text-Dependent Questions

1.  **Write enough questions.** When we first reduced our daily reading to excerpts of 500–1,000 words (versus three to four times that amount in our previous reading instruction), we struggled to come up with enough suitable questions. We didn't grasp how to create substantial questions for what seemed to be such a brief amount of content. Our inexperience in knowing how to use questioning within the context of close reading was telling. Once we better understood the objectives of our questions, things fell into place. We learned that by breaking apart paragraphs and sentences, by looking closely at word choice and the use of punctuation, our questions helped students take note of key details. We began using our questions by studying ideas in isolation and then reuniting them cohesively in a way that allowed students to extract new meaning not detectable through a cursory reading. Use your questions as tools to excavate the meaning of a passage.

2.  **Create specific questions.** Like our students, we had to dig deeply into a passage in order to grasp its deeper-level meaning to present in the context of close reading instruction. A cursory reading and generic questions could not hold up under the scrutiny of close reading. The specific content, structure, genre, and features of the passage matter greatly and are the essence of what is uncovered through purposeful text-dependent questions. There are no shortcuts. Ensure that your questions are of the same quality that is demanded of close reading.

3.  **Limit the number of questions.** Close reading is time sensitive, so it's best to limit your questions to three to four per daily reading segments. Early on, we thought that upward of five or six was feasible, but we soon found that the length of lessons did not allow us to cover the scope of the content. We weeded out questions that didn't support the substance of the segments, we refined questions we felt were beneficial to retain, and we considered other ways we might include them in our discussion. In each case, carefully reflecting on our own thinking made the questions that much stronger.

4.  **Focus on evidence in the text.** Although we knew that the text had to include evidence to support responses to our questions, it was difficult to keep our own knowledge and opinions from creeping into our questions. Be mindful to avoid this situation!

5. **Stick to the plan**. Questions that focus on author technique, structure, content, and other legitimate topics have a way of pulling instruction away from its charted course, so pacing your instruction is critical. You may have to move students along even if they want to linger on specific questions.

## Professional Development Activities

- Review the bulleted list on page 46 that describes parameters of text-dependent questions. Recall your own experiences creating questions and describe how your methods might change as you address your current standards.

- Using an excerpt from your professional development activities in Chapter 3 or from a well-known text you use for grade-level instruction, design three to five text-dependent questions using The 5 Keys of Composing Text-Dependent Questions Action Plan on page 50. Share your questions with colleagues, select the ones you feel will be most beneficial to students, and discuss the criteria you used in your selection.

- Compare and contrast the criteria you used in the activity above to the list of guiding questions on pages 52 and 53 in Case Study: Rigorous Review Using a Collaborative Approach. Determine if there are changes you want to make to the list of questions and then tailor them to suit your needs.

*Close Reading for the Whole Class* • © 2015 by Sandra K. Athans & Denise Ashe Devine • Scholastic Teaching Resources

**Sample Questions Aligned to the CCSS Reading Standards**

LITERATURE

## Key Ideas and Details

| Standard 1 | • Who, What, Where, Why, When questions<br>• What do you infer from the events in paragraph X? |
|---|---|
| Standard 2 | • Which statement best reflects the central message, lesson, or moral of the passage?<br>• How does the author convey the moral in the text?<br>• What is the theme of this passage?<br>• Which statement best summarizes the text?<br>• How does this challenging event steer the plot of the story? |
| Standard 3 | • How do the story elements, including character, setting, and events, enhance the message in the story?<br>• Which story element(s) is (are) central to the theme of the story?<br>• Compare and contrast the story elements, including characters, events, and setting in two or more passages. |

## Craft and Structure

| Standard 4 | • What is the best meaning of the word X as it is used in the story?<br>• Explain how the author's word choice contributes to the rhythm of the poem.<br>• What deeper-level meaning does the author intend through the idiom used in paragraph X?<br>• What does the author allude to in the phrase "Herculean effort"?<br>• How does the metaphor X enhance the meaning of the passage? |
|---|---|
| Standard 5 | • How does the sequence of events contribute to your understanding of the story?<br>• What is the contribution of stanza X in the poem?<br>• Compare and contrast X and Y (paired texts) based on their structural elements. |
| Standard 6 | • Identify each characters' view in regard to X (specific event).<br>• Does your personal point of view differ from the main character's perspective?<br>• How might this story be different if it were told in first person instead of third person?<br>• How did the character's past experiences influence his or her point of view? |

## Integration of Knowledge and Ideas

| Standard 7 | • Explain how illustrations support the text.<br>• How does the oral presentation of the speech affect you differently than the printed version?<br>• Analyze how visual and multimedia elements contribute to the meaning of the text. |
|---|---|
| Standard 8 | • Compare and contrast two versions of the same story.<br>• Compare and contrast the themes in two works by the same author.<br>• Compare and contrast the theme in the myths from two different cultures.<br>• Describe how the approach differs in these two mysteries. |

## Key Ideas and Details

| Standard 1 | • Who, What, Where, Why, When questions |
|---|---|
| Standard 2 | • Which statement best reflects the main idea of the passage?<br>• What is the main idea of this passage?<br>• Which statement best outlines the main idea of the text?<br>• Determine two or more main ideas in the text and explain how they are supported by the key details. |

## Craft and Structure

| Standard 3 | • What is the meaning of X (domain-specific word)? |
|---|---|
| Standard 4 | • How does the sidebar (or any text feature, such as caption, bold print, subheading, or hyperlink) add to the information provided in the passage?<br>• How is this passage organized and how does this organization help you better understand the passage?<br>• Compare and contrast X and Y (paired texts) based on their overall structure. |
| Standard 5 | • What was the author's purpose for writing this text?<br>• Do you agree or disagree with the author's perspective on this topic? How does your point of view differ?<br>• Compare the first- and second-hand accounts of this topic. |

## Integration of Knowledge and Ideas

| Standard 6 | • Explain how the images clarify the meaning of the text.<br>• Use information from the passage and the website to locate the answers to the following questions . . . |
|---|---|
| Standard 7 | • Which detail best supports the following statement (main idea)?<br>• How does the information in paragraph X support the idea(s) presented in the first paragraph?<br>• In the passage the author claims X. What evidence in the passage supports this claim?<br>• Compare and contrast the most important points about topic X presented in these two passages. |
| Standard 8 | • Describe (create a presentation about) what you have learned about the topic using information from both sources.<br>• Describe (create a presentation about) what you have learned about the topic using information from multiple sources. |

## Prioritizing the Essentials in "The Champion of Quiet"

These essentials go with the marked copy of "The Champion of Quiet" on page 43. Items considered a priority are starred. The rest of the items are reserved for discussion, taught outside of close reading, or omitted from instruction.

There must be a question asking why Maggie hates Tuesdays. This launches the problem in the story and is critical in analyzing story structure. Also, it's not hard to uncover. It's a good way to start small.

I love that "sandwiched" is used as a verb. It doesn't warrant a question, but I think it's deserving of a very brief chat about using context clues when we encounter atypical uses of familiar words.

The italics signal that Maggie is thinking. Students need to recognize this because it helps uncover the theme of the story. But it's not a pattern they'll recognize on Day 1—the evidence is too weak. I'll save it for a question on Day 2 when more examples appear.

"Champion" is a rich word that can be used as both a noun and a verb. It tells us that Maggie is a new student and uneasy. She tries to remember classmates by giving out nicknames. At the end of the story, she gets a "real" nickname. This is a critical path of analysis. I think I'll create a question that lingers a bit on the topic of nicknames and their role and importance.

"Maggie felt blue" is an idiom. My students have trouble with idioms. A question here will be a good check. Also, grasping that Maggie feels blue adds depth to the problem in the story. Maggie doesn't just "hate" Tuesdays, they make her feel sad because she's picked last. This will resonate with students. There is also an opportunity to extend our understanding of author intention here. We want our students to recognize that our ability to empathize with a character is often what draws us into a story.

Maggie's decision to use her voice is a critical point in the story. Students need to recognize the importance of this moment as we move through our Day 1 reading. I think it is deserving of a task.

I'm going to pass on "Tardy" as a vocabulary word. It doesn't contribute to the central meaning, and it can't be determined through context clues.

Jasmine is also "blue." I'm going to combine these ideas into a single question.

---

Text-dependent questions crafted after prioritizing the essentials and determining a path of analysis.

**Question 1:** What is Maggie's problem with Tuesdays? Use evidence from the passage to support your answer.

**Question 2:** What does the author convey in these sentences: "Maggie felt blue and . . . Jasmine seemed a little blue, too?" Support your response using evidence from the text.

**Question 3:** Why does Maggie nickname everyone "Champion of" something? Is she being mean? Support your ideas using text-based evidence.

# Chapter 5

# Performance Tasks

Performance tasks are essentially prompted activities that students complete as a part of their close reading instruction. They probe deeper than text-dependent questions, often requiring students to synthesize ideas and knowledge they construct from text-based questions. We use tasks sparingly—perhaps one task for every three or four questions—a ratio based on recommendations from our state education department. Tasks also test students' ability to integrate knowledge and ideas when comparing two or more passages, a requirement of most elementary grade-level standards. In these cases, tasks typically follow passages that have been completely read and discussed. In sum, tasks reflect a synthesis of ideas derived from segments of a passage or multiple passages.

Examples of performance tasks for grades 2–6 appear on pages 64 and 65. These are based on exemplars featured on many state education websites, including those of New York, Oregon, and California. There are slight differences between tasks used with literature and those used with informational texts, including those within the history/social studies disciplines in grades 6–8. These differences align with the structure of the CCSS. The skills emphasized in each task are also aligned to CCSS standards.

## Flexible Uses in the Classroom

Students can complete performance tasks on their own or with teacher support. Independently completed tasks can provide insights that can inform your instruction. For example, you might guide students through tasks, modeling reading behaviors, thinking processes, and written responses. Case Study: Identifying Theme or Main Idea below demonstrates how you can transition students toward independence using more complex performance tasks. Like text-based questions, performance tasks can be used flexibly, depending upon your objectives.

Performance tasks take anywhere from 5 to 25 minutes or more, depending upon the task, so you may opt to have students complete them outside of instructional time. Incorporating a task as morning work or independent work while you are conducting small-group instruction are other options.

## *Case Study:* Identifying Theme or Main Idea

We often ask students to identify the theme or main idea after we complete our close reading instruction of a passage. This is an effective final task because it allows us to gauge students' level of comprehension and their use of close reading skills. We read many of our passages over the span of several days, so we remind students to consider the passage as a whole. We encourage them to reflect upon, evaluate, and square their ideas with the author's intention. Students' use of evidence is another must. This is difficult for students at first, yet we help them with scaffolding.

We begin this task by summarizing key events, ideas, or points in the passage as a group. We typically move through the passage from start to finish, interjecting critical understandings we uncovered from questions or tasks we addressed earlier. We often refer to this as an "insightful" summary because it includes  important ideas that reflect our deeper-level thinking. Using open-ended phrases such as, "Although we weren't aware of the character's motive at the time, we later learned that . . ." We also ask questions that encourage students to consider the author's intentions, such as, "We feel the author deliberately included this to strengthen our understanding of the character's motive . . ." For informational text we might interject, "While much information was presented, we eventually learned that some of it was misinterpreted . . ." While considering an author's views we might add, "The author casts doubt by . . ." The routine asks students to complete the ideas or add support to the insightful summary, yet the pace is swift and guided by us.

We then step back from the text to look at it in a larger context: "If we look beyond the specifics in the story, the larger, more universal idea revealed to us by the author is . . ." We then help students shape the theme of the passage. We use this same approach for informational passages. We step away from the text and say, "The critical idea that the author suggests is . . ." and have students supply the answer.

By about the third or fourth passage, students get the hang of this process. At that point, we help them articulate their ideas in writing. Both move them toward independent mastery of the skill of identifying theme and main idea.

# Characteristics of Performance Tasks

Close reading performance tasks are often presented together with text-dependent questions. Both represent ways students interact with and respond to their reading, and both enable students to share and demonstrate knowledge.

## *Similarities Between Performance Tasks and Text-Dependent Questions*

Both reflect the objectives of close reading. Because the goal of close reading is to gain knowledge, performance tasks must let us see whether students have succeeded in reaching that goal. This idea seems simple, but teachers often miss it as they adjust and align their existing instructional materials. Tasks must do much more than simply ask students to perform a literacy-based activity; they must show that students have gained deep-level knowledge, or move them toward this goal in a manner that is consistent with the author's intentions.

Consider this example from a third-grade literature class, depicted in the chart on page 64:

*Determine the meaning of words and phrases in the poem, particularly focusing on identifying the poet's use of nonliteral language and talking about how it suggests meaning. (RL.3.4)*

In order for students to analyze the poet's use of figurative language, they must first construct a broad understanding of the poem. This task relies on deep-level reading, and it requires students to think about the poem as a whole.

We created the next task to use with "The Champion of Quiet," a fourth-grade close reading passage. It is similar to the exemplar above yet is text-specific.

**Task:** *In your own words, explain what Maggie means when she says, "Maybe it was time for the Champion of Quiet to use her voice." Use evidence from the passage to support your answer.*

Like the previous task, it also requires students to consider the meaning of the phrase within the context of the entire story.

⭐ **Performance tasks and questions both rely upon evidence from the passage.** The use of text-based evidence is critical, especially as students are reading, and rereading, more difficult passages and being asked to pay particular attention to how the evidence supports their inferences. Students' views must be on track with the author's intention. This experience is highlighted in most standards, and significantly affects how we reshape our thinking about acceptable levels of supporting details. It also affects the way in which we must prepare students to address it.

The example from the chart on page 65 asks sixth-grade students to cite text evidence for the inferences they make about the meaning of a text:

*Cite explicit textual evidence as well as draw inferences about the characters X and Y in Text A to support your analysis of the perils of selfishness. (RL.6.1)*

Helping students first locate and build clued evidence, which is evidence based on plausible clues in the text, is the first step in this task. Helping them articulate this evidence is the next step.

We created the following task for a third-grade-level close reading passage on natural weather disasters. It is similar to the exemplar above, except it asks students to make inferences based on visual information.

**Task:** *Look at the captions and photographs on pages 22–24. How do they support the main idea of the passage?*

Students locate clued evidence in the visuals and identify how it connects to the main idea of the passage.

⭐ **Performance tasks, like questions, must engage students.** All students must be encouraged to participate in this activity. To make our tasks engaging, we need to illuminate points within the text that deserve our attention, places that present us with a truth, a new or unique perspective, or a turning point. The example on page 64, for third-grade students, features this kind of illuminating analysis:

*Explain how the main idea that President X had "many faces" is supported by key details in the photobiography. (RI.3.2)*

The following task for fifth-grade students is based on excerpts from a speech delivered by Susan B. Anthony in 1873.

**Task:** *Susan B. Anthony compares the United States government to two other forms of government. Identify these forms and explain how they are different from a democracy.*

This task makes an interesting comparison between democracy and other forms of government and does so by drawing upon Anthony's compelling words.

## *Distinguishing Characteristics of Performance Tasks*

Tasks are well suited to the reading standards that call for comparisons. For example, some of the CCSS reading standards ask students to compare two or more texts. Tasks seem better suited for the depth and scope of analysis that these standards ask of students. The complexity of the skills they require means students will have to devote considerable time and energy to practice them, and it is likely that you will spend more time on tasks than on text-dependent questions. Students will typically work on tasks after close reading a given passage.

The following example demonstrates how CCSS Literature Standard 9 at the fourth-grade level can be translated into a task using paired passages.

**RL.4.9:** *Compare and contrast the treatment of similar themes and topics (e.g., opposition of good and evil) and patterns of events (e.g., the quest) in stories, myths, and traditional literature from different cultures.*

**Task:** *Compare and contrast Minli's quest in* Where the Mountain Meets the Moon *and Dorothy's quest in* The Wonderful Wizard of Oz. *Discuss key similarities and differences between the two, using evidence from both stories.*

☆ **Tasks make efficient use of technology.** Some standards require or suggest the use of technology. Be sure to incorporate technology in ways that align with the standards. Here, too, the scope of the analysis and the time commitment may be better suited to tasks. The following example demonstrates how CCSS Standard 7 for informational text can be addressed at the sixth-grade level:

- **RI.6.7:** *Integrate information presented in different media or formats (e.g., visually, quantitatively) as well as in words to develop a coherent understanding of a topic or issue.*

- **Task:** *After exploring a written text, a short video, and several pieces of artwork created during the time period of the Great Chicago Fire of 1871, discuss ways in which the weather, human error, and the close proximity of buildings contributed to the destruction caused by the fire. Use information from all sources in your response.*

☆ **Tasks can be used to address writing, speaking and listening, and language standards.** Learning to translate an oral response into a written response is a valuable skill that students need to acquire. Tasks can help support students' ability to articulate their ideas in writing and demonstrate their progress. Tasks can also allow you to better address the other categories of standards that compete for your instructional time. Academic discussions incorporate the speaking and listening standards, and tasks are a natural fit for addressing the writing standards.

CCSS Writing Anchor Standard 9 addresses the relationship between reading and writing across the grade levels (beginning in grade 4), yet you may use your close reading instruction in other ways. The following examples for grades 2, 4, and 6 demonstrate how CCSS Writing Anchor Standard 7 can be used across grade levels as a performance task. As you'll note, the examples for grades 2 and 4 demonstrate ways in which to scaffold student skills, while grade level 6 shows student-directed research.

**Writing Anchor Standard 7:** *Conduct short as well as more sustained research projects based on focused questions, demonstrating understanding of the subject under investigation.*

### Grade 2: Teacher-Assisted Research Project

***Research Task:*** *Animals help people in many ways. Read about and discuss three examples where animals have rescued people. Describe and record ways the rescues are similar and different. After your research, discuss what new idea(s) you would like to add to the statement: "Animals help people in many ways." Use a selection of two to three texts or passages such as* Animal Heroes: True Rescue Stories *by Sandra Markle and* Rescue Dogs *by Kristen Rajczak. Read aloud or have students read independently as appropriate. Guide discussion and record student ideas and comments.*

### Grade 4: Paired Research Project

***Research Task:*** *After reading and analyzing two related texts such as* Where the Mountain Meets the Moon *by Grace Lin and* Dragons and Serpents *by Gerrie McCall and Lisa Regan, think of a question or topic you and a partner would like to research further, based on your initial comparison of the two texts. Use approved*

*Internet or other school resources to help you write a research paper in support of your findings.* Students have already analyzed some similarities and differences between the two texts. This research task extends their understanding by using additional sources, which may include literature and/or informational texts.

**Grade 6: Self-Guided Research Project**
***Research Task:*** *The relationship between man and nature can be categorized in several ways: man helps nature, man hurts nature, nature helps man, and nature hurts man. After reading one of our mountaineering texts, such as* Tales From the Top of the World: Climbing Mount Everest With Pete Athans *by Sandra K. Athans (2013), extend your research on Mount Everest by focusing on one of the many ways the book depicts these four complex relationships. Present your findings to classmates using a format of your own choice.*

⭐ **Tasks can be used to assess students' progress in developing and building standards-based skills.**
Tasks can be one measure you use to evaluate students' progress. For instance, tasks can help you identify where targeted intervention or guided small-group instruction may be necessary. Perhaps a student correctly infers something about a text but is unable to identify clues in the passage that enabled him to do so. A written response prompt could reveal that distinguishing a good guess from a valid inference is a skill he needs to develop. Or a student may demonstrate a partial understanding of key ideas but not to the degree that enables her to pull those ideas together as evidence in support of the author's intention. This student's written response could reveal that she needs specific fix-up strategies.

Performance tasks can also be used to help students showcase and make substantial use of their earlier efforts to read and respond to questions analytically and deeply. Students have worked hard to comprehend complex text, and many will want to share this in a written task. Both you and your students will benefit from this final assessment as a way to monitor their progress and growth.

## Crafting Performance Tasks

Just as with crafting text-dependent questions, there are no unwavering rules for creating performance tasks. The examples in the charts on pages 64 and 65 and the examples in this chapter are simply good guides for shaping your own tasks.

Revisit The 5 Keys of Composing Text-Dependent Questions Action Plan on pages 50 and 51 for tips on when to create tasks. Text-dependent questions and tasks are interdependent, so it makes sense to create them at the same time. The exception is when you're helping students develop comparative skills by first reading multiple passages and then completing a comparative task. These types of tasks are better suited as final or culminating tasks.

Keys 1–3 remain the same for task development, as does Key 5; the only difference is that you will want to consider ways to coordinate your use of questions and tasks early on. Likewise, you will want to pay particular attention to the standards that may be better served by tasks and determine the best opportunities to include them.

# *Five Tips* for Creating Successful Performance Tasks

1. **Monitor your time and use it flexibly.** Performance tasks are involved. Students may respond in writing, use technology, make comparisons. Determine how best to use your instructional time and other time during the day so students don't feel rushed. They must feel as if they have the time to use their best effort and demonstrate their knowledge and abilities. Consider beginning a task in class and having students complete it at other times, such as during writing time, morning work, and so on. Think about your options and plan accordingly.

2. **Consider ways to best utilize your tasks.** The tasks you use might qualify as a form of documentation that your district requires, which can save you valuable time. For example, you might include tasks as a component of a student's portfolio or to fulfill a district writing requirement. Determining how your tasks can serve "double duty" will save time for you and your students. Discussing this option with the appropriate district personnel could result in a worthwhile savings of time and energy.

3. **Mix up your tasks, but don't forget to include complex standards.** Close reading instruction is something of a juggling act; on any given day, you may introduce a new skill, practice another skill, or work toward proficiency and mastery of other skills. Your tasks will reflect this. For example, tasks may help students interpret important idioms, transfer their knowledge of point of view to a new genre, and/ or evaluate their ability to compare and contrast story elements across cultural folktales. Planning diverse and selective tasks is important. Be sure to look for opportunities to include some of the more complex standards that are easy to overlook.

4. **Make sure a task assesses what you have in mind.** If you are working on text structure with your students, use a task to assess how well they understand text structure, not their knowledge of point of view. Although this seems evident, you'll want to keep it in mind as you create tasks.

5. **Supplement district-approved or packaged materials.** Although your district may require you to use approved instructional materials, determine if you have the flexibility to create tailored supplemental tasks. We use a selection of materials provided by our state education department, yet we often modify the tasks to better align with our students' needs.

## Professional Development Activities

▪ Using the text-dependent questions you created in the second activity on page 54, create three to five varied tasks using the guidelines and information presented in this chapter. Share your ideas with your colleagues.

▪ Create several tasks to address some of the CCSS or state comparison standards for your grade level. Consider a pair of texts, such as a classic and a favorite, that might present a good point of comparison for your students.

▪ Discuss ways you might use a written task to help fulfill your district's documentation requirements. Share your ideas with colleagues.

# Examples of Close Reading Performance Tasks for Grades 2–5

| Grade Level | Performance Tasks for Stories, Drama, and Poetry | Performance Tasks for Informational Text |
|---|---|---|
| **Grades 2–3**<br><br>*(Some tasks at these grade levels are based on read-aloud stories.)* | • Ask and answer questions regarding the plot of Text A, explicitly referring to the book to form the basis for answers. (RL.3.1)<br>• Paraphrase the central message, lesson, or moral from Text A (cultural fable/folktale). (RL.2.2)<br>• Describe the overall story structure of Text A, describing how the interactions of the characters introduce the beginning of the story and how the suspenseful plot comes to an end. (RL.2.5)<br>• Determine the meaning of words and phrases in the poem, particularly focusing on identifying the poet's use of nonliteral language and talking about how it suggests meaning. (RL.3.4)<br>• Explain how the illustrations in Text A contribute to what is conveyed in the text and help create mood and emphasize aspects of characters and setting in the story. (RL.3.7) | • Describe the reasons behind the author's statement that bird migration is a survival behavior and how she uses those points in the text. (RI.2.8)<br>• Identify what the author wants to answer in Text A and explain the main purpose of the text. (RI.2.6)<br>• Explain how the main idea that President X, had "many faces" in the photobiography is supported by key details in the text. (RI.3.2)<br>• Use text features, such as the table of contents and headers, in Text A to identify relevant sections and locate information related to a given topic. (RI.3.5)<br>• Using your understanding of how cause and effect gives order to events, include specific language to describe the sequence of events that leads to event X. (RI.3.3) |
| **Grades 4–5** | • Describe how the narrator's point of view in Text A influences how events are described and how the reader perceives the main character. (RL.5.6)<br>• Summarize the plot of Text A and then reflect on the challenges facing the characters, while employing these and other text details to discuss the value of inquisitiveness and exploration of the story's theme. (RL.5.2)<br>• Determine the meaning of the metaphor in Text A and explain how the use of this figurative language supports and advances the plot. (RL.4.4)<br>• Describe in depth the idyllic setting in Text A, drawing on specific details in the text. (RL.4.3)<br>• Explain the selfish behavior of Character A by explicitly referring to details and examples from the text. (RL.4.1) | • Explain how the author uses reasons and evidence to support particular points regarding the topology of the plant. (RI.4.8)<br>• Identify the overall structure of ideas, concepts, and information in Text A and compare and contrast that scheme to Text B. (RI.5.5)<br>• Interpret the meaning of domain-specific words or phrases in Text A. (RI.4.4)<br>• Determine the main idea of Text A and create a summary by explaining how key details support the author's view. (RI.4.2)<br>• Compare and contrast a firsthand and a secondhand account of major events in Text A and Text B, attending to the focus of each account and the information provided in each. (RI.4.6) |

*Close Reading for the Whole Class* • © 2015 by Sandra K. Athans & Denise Ashe Devine • Scholastic Teaching Resources

# Examples of Close Reading Performance Tasks for Grade 6

| Grade Level | Performance Tasks for Stories, Drama, and Poetry | Performance Tasks for Informational Text | Performance Tasks for History/Social Studies and Science, Mathematics, and Technical Subjects (These examples span grades 6–8.) |
|---|---|---|---|
| Grade 6 | • Cite explicit textual evidence as well as draw inferences about the characters X and Y in Text A to support your analysis of the perils of selfishness. (RL.6.1)<br>• Explain how the playwright uses particular elements of drama (e.g., setting and dialogue) to create dramatic tension in play X. (RL.6.3)<br>• Explain how the author's choice of words develops the point of view of the young speaker in text A. (RL.6.6) | • Trace the line of argument in X's address to Parliament and evaluate his specific claims and opinions in the text, distinguishing which claims are supported by facts, reasons, and evidence, and which are not. (RI.6.8)<br>• Analyze in detail how the early years of this abolitionist's life (as portrayed by the author) contributed to her later becoming a conductor on the Underground Railroad, attending to how the author introduces, illustrates, and elaborates upon the events in the abolitionist's life. (RI.6.3)<br>• Determine the figurative and connotative meaning of the author's choice of words and phrases in the text, and analyze how this word choice impacts the meaning and tone of the writing. (RI.6.4) | • Analyze the governmental structure of the U.S. by citing specific textual evidence from primary sources and secondary sources. (RH.6–8)<br>• Describe how the author of Text A integrates and presents information both sequentially and causally to explain the civil rights movement. (RH. 6–8)<br>• Compare and contrast the information contained in Text A with the multimedia sources available at Site X. (RH.6–8) |

# Academic Discussions

The outcome of our revamped discussion practices came as a surprise to us. What we learned was that discussion—as an instructional tool—can have a significant effect on how students explore text. Through discussion, we tackled tough topics head-on and forged through dense material we might previously have simplified or avoided altogether. The text-dependent questions and performance tasks we so carefully prepared led the way. Typically, we have in mind a range of acceptable responses; yet, as students developed skills in the effective use of evidence, making inferences, and building well-supported ideas, their discourse grew stronger and often shaped our discussions. We also learned that the success of our close reading activities for our struggling readers often depended upon the effectiveness of our discussions.

## How Discussion Supports Close Reading

In the past, our discussions were largely teacher-directed, comprised of finite questions that a small subset of the class answered. These would no longer even qualify as discussions. Today, we use a variety of grouping configurations, including paired groups, small clusters of three to five students, and whole class. Through such groupings, students learn to help one another build an understanding of complex texts and develop skills that will eventually be applied independently.

Small-group configurations foster students' ability to explore complex texts. When students practice with and learn from classmates during group discussion, they gain access to peer support networks, a type of authentic scaffold that, in our experience, is highly beneficial. Additionally, varied grouping strategies provide insights into students' thinking, enabling you to provide targeted support and plan future instruction. The variety of discussion formats reveals who knows how to distinguish main ideas from supporting details, who struggles to identify themes in multicultural folklore, and who firmly grasps the different structures found in informational passages. You can also detect how students shape ideas, formulate inferences, and monitor their own thinking—insights that are key to helping you provide support and guide ongoing close reading instruction.

The chart on the next page features some targets that we expect to see and hear as we observe our students in close reading discussions. These targets are indicators of successful performance and show how the reading standards work together with other standards to build students' skills and abilities. You can return to these guidelines as you adjust your discussion practices and as you monitor your students during discussions.

**Discussion Targets**

| Behaviors (Watch-for Targets) | Discussions (Listen-for Targets) |
|---|---|
| • Contribute<br>• Be prepared<br>• Take turns<br>• Follow procedures and protocols<br>• Maintain attentiveness and focus<br>• Express interest in others' ideas through questions, comments, and remarks<br>• Return often to the text passage<br>• Text mark, highlight, or write down new or important ideas<br>• Encourage and support one another<br>• Demonstrate stamina | • Clarify their understanding of the question under discussion<br>• Share views and interpretations of the text that reflects thoughtful and critical thinking<br>• Discuss the meaning of vocabulary words<br>• Address skills and strategies that are featured in the reading standards<br>• Break apart and interpret sections of the passage: sentences, lines, stanzas, subsections<br>• Support ideas with text evidence<br>• Distinguish inferences and support them with text evidence<br>• Agree with peers and articulate evidence-based reasoning<br>• Disagree skillfully with peers and articulate evidence-based reasoning<br>• Express original ideas and reasoning to a group<br>• Express group ideas and reasoning to a larger group<br>• Encourage and support one another |

## Close Reading Discussions: The Multipurpose Tool

We regard close reading discussion as a multipurpose tool. It helps us teach critical and analytical reading skills, informs how we identify what our students need, and helps define how we should target our instruction. We can even use discussion to monitor our success in all of these endeavors, as we discuss below.

✬ **Grouping Students for Discussions:** You can group students for discussions in pairs, small groups of three to five students, or as a whole class. Another option is the "think-pair-share" model, where students work independently and then move to small groups and possibly to larger-group sharing. You might even use all three groupings, shifting from one to another based on a variety of factors and your objectives. For example, some teachers choose the small-group model for the first two days of a three-day lesson and then move to a whole-class model to conclude the lesson. They hope to maximize the benefits of small-group dynamics, including diverse thinking, a variety of skills, and a larger peer support network. Or a teacher might choose to rely on the paired model for the entire three-day lesson to maximize participation.

Careful planning of pairs and small groups is vital to addressing students' diverse needs. For example, you might create balanced groups in which students with similar skills and abilities can provide helpful peer support to struggling learners. Or you might pair a strong reader with a developing reader, keeping in mind that paired groups share with other paired groups. All students benefit from the larger peer-support network. Certainly, you can create groups of varying sizes, too. Making the best use of your students' diverse strengths by planning your groups carefully is a skill that develops over time, as you explore the nature and depth of the close reading discussions, and as you become familiar with your students. Determining which grouping structure works best is up to you.

# Introducing Students to Discussions

After establishing your grouping scheme, you're ready to launch discussion groups. No matter which configuration you choose, students need to be taught the basics of an effective, productive discussion. They should understand your expectations and objectives and what authentic discussions look and sound like.

A Take-5 Mini-Lesson Plan for introducing discussions into your classroom appears on pages 74 and 75. The mini-lesson features brief dialogue prompts and action cues that you can easily adapt to reflect your classroom practices and instructional style. "Follow-Through Tips" provide ideas you can embed into your main lesson, and "Extending the Skill" list suggestions to enhance student learning beyond the mini-lesson. As you deliver your mini-lesson, be sure to expand upon how these discussions will help everyone improve their deeper-level understanding of a reading passage. Explain that students will do the following in discussions with peers:

- Think through questions and contribute ideas
- Listen to and consider the views of others
- Remain attentive and responsive while the class builds ideas through the discussion process

The reward of working through ideas and arriving at a well considered understanding is an appreciation of knowledge itself, and the process of gaining it.

Asking students to help create a list of discussion protocols supports their ownership of the process and can be a good start-up activity. Your students all have varying degrees of experience with discussions, so tap this knowledge to generate a quick working list of ground rules. They can contribute a few ideas beneath each category and keep adding to the list as they become experienced in discussions and close reading. It may be necessary to clarify that some protocols reflect observable behaviors, while others identify mental processes. Point out that close reading discussions differ from other forms of discussion in their use of evidence, consideration of author intent, deep analysis, and so on.

You can use your authentic classroom experiences to express, clarify, and model your expectations for discussions. If you feel that some matters are too important to leave to chance, create special protocols for them. For example, if you want to ensure that a speaker has a comfortable amount of time to express an idea before others respond to it, you may want to break in to or pause the lesson to explain the expectation and model the behavior, as well as embed authentic opportunities for students to practice in future lessons.

The idea that good discussions rely on responsive listening is another matter that often requires direct instruction and practice. We've all been in classrooms where a succession of students responds to a question in an identical manner. This experience is painful for everyone! Although someone may share an idea that is similar to a classmate's, encouraging acknowledgement of that is the first step in guiding students to stretch their thinking and contribute something new. This begins the exchange of ideas, which is the hallmark of good discussion. One strategy to facilitate discussion is to help students express how their ideas square with, or differ from, those expressed by their classmates. Here are three variations of discussion stems to share with students:

- *I agree with X and would like to add . . .*
- *I agree with X, but for different reasons. My thinking is . . .*
- *I agree mostly with X, but I disagree with his or her views on . . . Instead, . . .*

We've found that students get this right away and are quick to construct their own ways of expressing these ideas. Students' ability to refine, reshape, and expand their reasoning so their contributions will add value to a group discussion begins with good listening skills.

Some students might need your help in expressing their ideas in a group discussion. Just as you assist students in fitting their ideas into those that have already been shared, you might also need to help them shape and express their ideas coherently. Most students can benefit from this type of support. The discussion stems that follow can help you restate the ideas expressed by a student or prompt a student to produce a response.

- *Can I help clarify your ideas about . . .?*
- *Can I help shape your thinking about . . .?*
- *Can I help connect the ideas you've expressed about . . .?*
- *Can I help recap your points about . . .?*
- *Can I help highlight the key ideas you've raised about . . .?*

The idea is not to put words in the students' mouth but to help them express their thinking.

## Whole-Class Stamina: Balancing Content Coverage, Pacing, and Engagement

Your students' stamina is a changeable thing that can quickly run out like sand in an hourglass. Helping students exchange ideas instead of repeating them is one way to help maintain their stamina—so is guiding them in shaping ideas as they find their voice and keeping a close eye on your pacing. Some other techniques for getting the most from your discussions include the following:

⭐ **Table the Topic:** This technique is useful for many circumstances: Your discussion isn't going anywhere; students require more scaffolding to participate effectively; a disagreement on the topic warrants more discussion; and so on. There is no harm in postponing a discussion until circumstances can be worked out, a new plan of action devised, or some other activity is put into place.

⭐ **Interject Ideas:** If the discussion is lagging or stalling, add a new idea and ask students for their reaction. Keep in mind that you only wish to jump-start the discussion, not monopolize it. This can be especially helpful with difficult topics. For example, students may require help in broaching terrible events that occur in Greek mythology. "Do you find it unusual that X ate his children?" is the kind of icebreaker that can launch a good discussion.

⭐ **Move to a Different Venue (Time and Place):** You have limited time to introduce ideas or concepts that will lead to deeper understanding (even though the passages are short segments of text). If some students are unable to grasp ideas, move the discussion to another time and place when you can meet with them independently. A one-on-one conversation or talking with a group of students may be the best course of action.

⭐ **Take Language Arts Instructional Discussion Outside:** Encouraging creative, thinking-outside-the-box discussion is a good thing, but it can be costly in terms of time and whole-class stamina. Still, you can encourage students to continue their discussions outside of the immediate language arts instructional time. Lunchtime, recess, and waiting-for-the bus discussions present good opportunities for students to share ideas.

⭐ **Know When Your Discussion Begins to Lose Value:** This speaks for itself. Know when it's time to move on!

## Keeping Discussions Focused

Despite diligent planning, you can't always predict the direction your close reading discussion may take. This is both good and bad. It's good if your discussion leads to an exchange of engaging and authentic ideas that remain focused on topic—and you've allotted time for this rich exchange of ideas.

Discussions that go off topic in one way or another have some value, but to save valuable class time, they should be tabled for later or taken outside of the language arts instructional time. It takes some finesse and diplomacy to keep things on track, especially as students are in the midst of learning new skills in close reading and in the art of discussion. Redirecting them carefully is often very difficult: You must attempt to juggle constructive criticism with encouragement—swiftly and at a moment's notice. Skilled diplomacy is what's needed.

Mastering the On-the-Fly Discussion Prompts for Close Reading on pages 76 and 77 can help you keep exchanges on track, evidence-based, focused, and sprinkled with heartfelt redirection.

# Facilitating a Discussion From Beginning to End

To support close reading instruction, you'll have multiple mini-discussions that dig deeply into the section of text you're reading or a question or task you're covering. It may be helpful to think of each mini-discussion as a process that begins one way, transforms, and comes to an end, almost as if it were following a life cycle. Although many factors will make each discussion unique, gauging how to nurture students through this process advantageously is a skill that develops with time and practice as you build know-how with the skills in this chapter. Pointers about the "life cycle" of a discussion are provided below.

## A Focused and Purposeful Beginning

The carefully constructed questions you prepare serve as the starting point for valuable class discussions. As you learned in Chapter 3, the questions encourage students to notice, evaluate, and support their understanding of critical ideas in a passage. The questions also appear in a sequence in order to scaffold students' construction of meaning. Getting off to a good, strong start with every question is critical.

Determine if each question launches a good beginning discussion by asking yourself questions like the following:

- Do students understand the question?
- Does the question produce discussion that helps guide students toward a cohesive understanding of the passage?
- Is the question producing a discussion that follows in a logical order?

You can quickly determine the answer to any of these questions by listening in on students who are having brainstorming discussions. If students misinterpret a question, you have several options. You could recall a similar question and discussion from an earlier passage, if one exists (see the "7-second-scaffold" on page 79.) As an alternative, you can stop and clarify the question. You might even choose to let students grapple with the question collaboratively as a way to reinforce their problem-solving skills. Determining your course of action will depend on the prior skills you've taught your students and your objectives.

**A word of caution:** If your discussion gets sidetracked and is not helping students build a cohesive understanding as a result of a misunderstanding or misguided analysis, and it takes too long to redirect focus, you may need to refine your questions at that moment. By carefully creating your questions, you can avoid this situation most of the time.

Then again, an incorrect answer can pave the way for a great discussion. Being able to identify such moments is key. As an example, a passage that appears in the second unit we cover early in the year presents information on folktales. One of the first things we ask of students is to identify the genre of the passage and to support their response with text evidence. Many identify the passage as a folktale or fiction and use the definition of the genre in the passage to support their claim. Although this response is incorrect, students did not misinterpret the question; they just got it wrong. They missed the point that the passage was an informational text that presented information about folktales. The discussion that surrounded this question was rich and rewarding *because* students initially answered it incorrectly. The resulting discussion helped them differentiate between the genres and to read more carefully.

## An Impromptu Middle

A strong, purposeful beginning helps to keep the next stage of your discussion from straying off course. In this middle phase, nurture the discussion by encouraging students to follow the ideas shared by their classmates and to react in a way that reflects their awareness.

In the above example, there are multiple avenues to take. Get students to describe how they arrived at one answer and not another by asking questions such as the following:

*Why do you think this is an informational text and not a folktale?*

*Did you think it was a folktale and then change your mind? If so, what led you to change your mind?*

*Why were you absolutely certain it wasn't a folktale?*

The prompts on pages 76 and 77 encourage students to use evidence and consider author intention effectively.

## The Wrap-It-Up and Move-Along Ending

Each discussion needs a strong ending. Based on what has been discussed, the finale might be a single statement that highlights an answer and/or the evidence used to support an answer. It could also be a broad overview of key ideas raised throughout the discussion. Then again, it might capture an essential idea that in some way has helped students gain a deeper understanding and appreciation of the passage. For example, you might conclude the above discussion on the misinterpreted genre by stating, "The insight we've uncovered here is that facts and details about a type of fiction, such as a folktale, should still be classified as a type of informational text."

# Timing

How much time you spend discussing a question depends on the value you place on it. Is the discussion helping students grasp a tricky or challenging area of the text? Does the discussion enable students to bridge their understanding and arrive at a deeper level of understanding? Is there value in extending the discussion, or has it reached its level of usefulness? If so, let it go. Determining the length of discussion for each question is a knack you develop over time. It's easy to let discussions go on for too long, so stay focused on keeping your students engaged!

# Brainstorming Discussions to Support Struggling Students

Brainstorming discussions, which can take place any time during the lesson, may precede formal discussions and are often rudimentary. They will become more refined as the group or pair shapes them into a more listener-reading, whole-class idea. Monitoring your students as they talk over ideas before discussions will give you insights into their skills, as well as provide you with a chance to extend their thinking and check their use of evidence through challenges and questions. During this time, you can also help struggling readers make connections and see how strategies can lead them to understand a tricky passage. You can use the On-the-Fly Discussion Prompts for Close Reading on pages 76 and 77 to support these students during these pre-discussion brainstorming sessions.

# Independent Discussions

The ultimate goal is for students to navigate these discussions independently, once they've gained confidence and can apply the skills and strategies described in this chapter. During our close reading instruction, we look for opportunities to let students facilitate their own peer discussions. These opportunities are best triggered authentically. For example, your discussion may take an unexpected turn based on a student's probing question. Invite discourse and debate on the question. Comment on the responses so students can understand the value of authentic questioning; for example: "This was a good question to explore because it helped us analyze X. It's likely that some of you may have had the same or a similar question." After students are comfortable with determining valuable, probing questions, we encourage them to create their own questions for selected reading passages. At first, we don't limit their questions. Encouraging students to explore all questions in a timely manner is a way for them to begin to distinguish which probe for deeper-level meaning and which concern cursory information in the passage.

# *Five Tips* for Successful Academic Discussions

1. **Redirect runaway discussions.** To help students get back on track, try some of the redirecting prompts pages 76 and 77. Over time, most students will develop self-monitoring skills and be able to realign or rein in their comments and contributions. As you redirect a discussion, keep in mind that you're not only improving the quality of the discussion, but you're also modeling beneficial behaviors for students so they can assume responsibility for their own discussions.

2. **Jump-start stalled discussions.** Signs that a discussion has become unproductive include inattentiveness, disengagement, lack of participation, and even frustration. Students' body language can be very telling. Although we want students to develop academic fortitude, there comes a point of diminishing returns when you must step in and move the discussion along by guiding them toward an answer. You can do this by narrowing the location of evidence, breaking down the task further, adding another question, and so on.

3. **Build masterful teacher feedback skills.** Knowing how to say something is just as important as knowing what to say. Be aware of the tone of your comments. Guide students with gentle directions such as, "I hope you didn't get tricked by . . ." or "If you're stumped, maybe you can find clues elsewhere in the passage . . ." Keeping a positive, encouraging, and enthusiastic tone is a way to acknowledge the struggle that might accompany a complex passage, and that the struggle is a valuable part of the process.

4. **Manage discussion time wisely.** Determining whether you're spending too much or too little time on discussions can be tough to gauge. It's important to be flexible so you can get your timing just right. You will always have to weigh the value of unplanned discussion against your intention of moving through a specified number of questions and tasks. Be open to this kind of learning opportunity, yet be prepared to justify how you can adjust your plans to stay on track.

5. **Use flexible grouping.** The ways in which you group students for discussion matters. Whether your goal is to support struggling learners or to have all students benefit from diverse group thinking, asking pairs or small clusters of students to brainstorm ideas prior to contributing to whole-class discussion is a helpful option.

## Professional Development Activities

- Devise a plan for three different ways to group your students for discussion. Assess the value of each and share your ideas with colleagues.

- Stage a close reading lesson with several of your colleagues and practice using some of the prompt techniques presented in this chapter. Consider ways to adjust the prompts to make them your own, and/or add your own ideas to those provided.

- Using information in this chapter, summarize the importance of class discussions in terms of close reading objectives. Discuss how you might change current discussion practices to maximize their effectiveness during your close reading instruction.

# *Mini-Lesson Plan:* Introducing Academic Discussions

**Objective:** To introduce academic discussions

**Delivery Suggestion:** Early Core Lesson

**Essential Question:** How can academic discussions help us build close reading skills?

**Guiding Questions:**

- What is an academic discussion?
- How is it used?
- Why is it used?

- What's the plan?
- How do students participate?

## Introduction

**Note:** You may want to use a method of formative assessment to ensure that students follow your ideas. "Thumbs up, if you understand," and so on.

*Academic discussions are a way we can share our thinking and our ideas out loud. We use the term "academic" because these discussions are about topics we're learning about and texts we're reading. Academic discussions are useful because they help us shape our deep thinking—the kind we use for close reading. They do this in two ways:*

1. *They force us to think our ideas through carefully so our classmates can understand them.*
2. *By listening to our classmates' ideas, we find ways to revise our own.*

*We use discussions during our close reading lessons by sharing our thinking about the questions and tasks (which we learned about earlier in our close reading lesson). Sometimes our discussions help us answer them, and other times we might discuss ideas that extend beyond them.*

*Your role is to participate in the discussions. You'll contribute ideas, listen to others' ideas, and then build deeper understandings based on this exchange of ideas. Throughout this lesson, we'll explore how to use discussions. You'll share with an elbow partner, then in small-table clusters, and finally, you'll share ideas with the whole class.*

**Optional Start-Up Activity:** Have students help create discussion protocols. You may want to use the anchor chart below as a time-saver.

*Let's get started by brainstorming a short list of discussion protocols, or helpful rules, that we can begin using today. We can add new ideas to the chart as we learn how to make good use of this tool in our classroom. (After a few minutes of recording ideas, direct students to the close reading lesson.)*

---

### Close Reading Discussions Anchor Chart

*Ways to share our ideas about topics we're studying and texts we're reading.*

1. Participate effectively
2. Treat classmates respectfully
3. Commit to using your best effort
4. Build your discussion skill and know-how
5. Support others in their learning experience

---

**Follow-Through Tips:** As you move through the questions and tasks during your planned close reading lessons, use various forms of discussions: partner, table, whole class. When necessary, break in to the lesson to explain and model some of your expectations or to assist students. See common break-in moments in the chart below.

| Break-in or Pause Moments | Dialogue Prompts |
|---|---|
| Wait Time | *Have you noticed how some of us aren't able to finish our thoughts? Some of us are eager to react to a classmate's ideas and may not realize that we're interrupting him or her. Even though it's unintentional, this doesn't seem respectful. Maybe we need a protocol to help us monitor our eagerness to respond too quickly. Are there suggestions?* |
| Responsive Listening | *Sometimes you might have an idea that is similar to one or more of your classmates' ideas. When this happens, let us know (rather than repeating the same response), but also challenge yourself to stretch your thinking and contribute something new. For example, you might say:*<br>• *I agree with X and would like to add . . .*<br>• *I agree with X, but for different reasons. My thinking is . . .*<br>• *I agree mostly with X, yet disagree with his/her views on. Instead, . . .*<br>*Maybe we can add a protocol for this.* |
| Helping Students Express Their Ideas | You may want to help students express their ideas, especially as they explore complex ideas that parallel their close reading. This support helps build confidence and encourages risk taking. Asking permission with "Can I...?" phrases lets a student know that he or she owns and retains rights to the idea, even though you may assist.<br>• *Can I help clarify your ideas about . . . ?*<br>• *Can I help shape your thinking . . . ?*<br>• *Can I help connect the ideas you've expressed . . . ?*<br>• *Can I help recap your points . . . ?*<br>• *Can I help highlight the key ideas you've raised?* |

**Extending the Skill:** You may want to break in to or pause a lesson and assign student Discussion Directors (one per table) to facilitate a discussion. Gently supporting their classmates' use of the protocols will give all students a helpful experience. This should be a rotating position.

**Closing the Planned Lesson:** *Now that we've completed today's close reading lesson, let's return to our Take-5 Mini-Lesson and share a couple of thoughts about the way we used discussion to build our close reading skills. I observed students participating and contributing.* (Share a few examples.) *These examples and others show me that you're getting a handle on how to use discussion effectively. Who would like to share his or her thoughts?*

# On-the Fly-Discussion Prompts for Close Reading

## Digging Deeply Into the Author's Intentions[1]

How does the author:

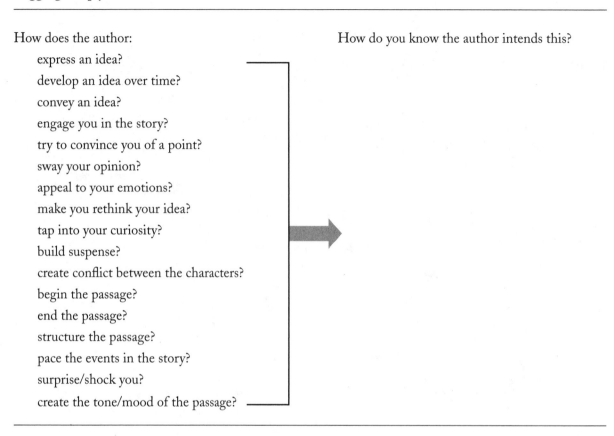

How do you know the author intends this?

- express an idea?
- develop an idea over time?
- convey an idea?
- engage you in the story?
- try to convince you of a point?
- sway your opinion?
- appeal to your emotions?
- make you rethink your idea?
- tap into your curiosity?
- build suspense?
- create conflict between the characters?
- begin the passage?
- end the passage?
- structure the passage?
- pace the events in the story?
- surprise/shock you?
- create the tone/mood of the passage?

What is the author trying to convey?

What key ideas does the author emphasize?

What motivates the author to include or exclude certain ideas and features?

What details does the author highlight?

What level of importance does the author place on an idea or a topic?

What techniques does the author use to present information?

What techniques does the author use to express an idea?

Why does the author create uncertainty?

Why has the author included questions?

Why has the author presented an idea in this manner?

Why has the author selected one method over another to convey information?

Why has the author used specific words/examples to express an idea?

---

[1] Although some of these prompts may seem similar, nuances in terms or in the manner in which they are expressed may distinguish their use within the range of diverse materials you use for close reading (e.g., excerpted text from a novel, or illustrated magazine narratives or articles).

## Use of Evidence Prompts

What details support your response?

Is your inference well supported with text-based evidence?

What evidence supports your inference?

Is there other evidence that supports your inference?

Does your interpretation square with the evidence?

Is your interpretation supported by evidence?

Is your interpretation cohesive?

Are your views supported throughout the passage?

How reliable are the details that support your response?

Are there multiple pieces of evidence to support your ideas?

What is the strongest evidence supporting your view?

Is there evidence that challenges your ideas?

## Redirecting or Digging Deeper Prompts

Have you considered other points of view?

Is there stronger evidence to support another view?

How well does your answer square with the author's intention?

Does your reasoning square with other details in the text?

Could there be a deeper level of meaning?

How can you stretch your thinking beyond this?

Would you consider rethinking your idea based on new evidence?

Could this cause you to refine your response?

How do you think others might respond?

Is your response influenced by text-based evidence?

Does your thinking hold up in all cases?

# Chapter 7

## Close Read Guides: A Nifty Tool for Instruction

Close Read Guides are simple tools you can create that pull together everything needed for close reading instruction: passages, text-based questions, and performance tasks. With everything in one place, you can deliver lessons efficiently, and students can follow instruction easily. It's no wonder that teachers who have attended our workshops call these nifty tools "the missing link" because they help bridge the gap between what should happen (the theory of close reading instruction) and what will feasibly work in today's classroom (the practice of close reading instruction). Samples from a fourth-grade Close Read Guide that we introduce at the beginning of the year appear on pages 88–90.

### The Benefits of Theme-Based Units

Close Read Guides unite reading materials into thematic instructional units. Using related passages to help students grasp, practice, and then independently apply the strategies and techniques for deep, analytical reading is a subtle form of scaffolding. The theme is the glue that holds the passages, questions, and tasks together and brings cohesion to your instruction.

Without this cohesion, connecting new close reading experiences to known experiences can be a choppy and time-consuming process. We have learned that students are better able to retrieve, connect, and transfer concepts within materials that share a common thread. When passages are grouped together, each one becomes a helpful resource to use for the instruction of the following passage. We playfully refer to this process with students as a "7-second scaffold" because that's typically the amount of time it takes to clinch a point when referencing an earlier passage in the unit.

### Compiling and Assembling a Close Read Guide

There are five steps in compiling and assembling a Close Read Guide.
**STEP 1:** Select a theme.
**STEP 2:** Compile the mix of passages.
**STEP 3:** Create questions and tasks.
**STEP 4:** Evaluate the mix of standards.
**STEP 5:** Create a culminating activity.

## The Process of Compiling a Close Read Guide

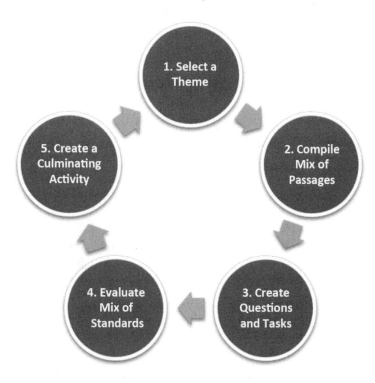

## Step 1: Select a Theme

One of the most significant lessons we've learned from our classroom experience is that we can fit roughly six to eight themed units into a school year, an average of less than one unit a month. As a starting point, plan for six to eight units (even though you probably won't have the time to complete all of them in your first year.)

The critical question becomes, *How do you determine* <u>*purposeful*</u> *themes for these close reading units?* We use the following criteria, some of which are similar to the guidelines for selecting text passages in Chapter 3:

Align themes to available materials
>    Align themes to content-area curriculum (science, social studies, math)
>    Consider criteria within the reading and other standards
>    Consider current and high-interest topics
>    Consider what's happening at other grade levels

What's important to note is that we use all five criteria to create a meaningful mix of themes. For example, when we assembled our first unit, we had little time to locate material and we had no available funds for new purchases. So we used passages that were readily available to us. We also tried to select passages that had survived the 5S Teacher Read process described in Chapter 3. After launching our first theme, we then used the other criteria to build and shape our thematic mix. Our results appear below.

### Theme 1: Accepting Ourselves and Others
>    Essential Question: *How do our feelings about ourselves affect us and others?*
### Theme 2: Our Big World
>    Essential Question: *In what ways are past and present cultures meaningful to us?*

**Theme 3: Mythology**

　　Essential Question: *Why has ancient Greek and Roman mythology withstood the test of time?*

**Theme 4: Colonial Times**

　　Essential Question: *How did families overcome hardships during colonial times?*

**Theme 5: Between the Lines** (poetry)

　　Essential Question: *How does an author communicate his or her ideas?*

**Theme 6: From Past to Present**

　　Essential Question: *How does our nation's past affect us today?*

**Theme 7: Our Changing World**

　　Essential Question: *How am I a part of this changing world?*

**Theme 8: New York and the Civil War, Immigration, and the Erie Canal**

　　Essential Question: *How has our search for freedom, our hope for prosperity, and our call for change, shaped us today?*

The last three themes fall at the end of the school year and encourage students to generate their own questions, apply close reading strategies, and comprehend text deeply and analytically.

At the outset, we roughly sketched out our ideas for all eight themes so we could integrate proven materials into our Close Read Guides. We also flagged potential passages we encountered during our routine classroom activities and monitored the guides' effectiveness to determine how to strengthen them. As we grew more knowledgeable of the standards and located more materials, we saw other ways to refine the guides.

If your district uses essential questions, you might want to draft very broad questions that reflect the direction you'd like your Close Read Guides to take from the start. You can always alter them as your guides take shape. As an alternative, you might wait to devise essential questions for a guide after you've selected your passages, created text-questions and performance tasks, and determined a culminating activity.

☆ **Align themes to available materials:** Selecting passages and a unit theme may happen simultaneously. In Chapter 3, you learned that one way to begin selecting passages is to review materials you already have (provided they align with grade-level complexity criteria). You can create themes around these materials.

We initially selected the theme for the sample Close Read Guide because we had materials readily available, but we have continued using it for other reasons. Students are drawn to characters with whom they share an experience—overcoming a challenge, recognizing a new skill or strength, befriending someone who is different, or building self-confidence and self-esteem. This theme is compelling and fits well with our early efforts to build classroom community.

If your state education department makes instructional materials available, you might sift through them for an appropriate passage to repurpose for a Close Read Guide. As an example, New York State features downloadable instructional modules for grades K–12, through Engage New York (www.engageny.org). Seasoned teachers use their professional judgment to determine what to include within their instruction and how to deliver it. This pick-and-choose repurposing strategy enables you to bypass scripted prompts and activities for your own time-tested tools and techniques. Newer teachers who feel they would benefit from more support may choose to use state-supplied materials in other ways within their language arts instruction. Alternately, you may choose to simply pair up with a more seasoned or a less experienced teacher for informal mentoring.

☆ **Align themes to content-area curriculum:** Another approach is to look at your curriculum and identify themes that align with your social studies and science instruction. Covering topics in these subject areas *and* through your close reading instruction is a way to "double-dose" students' exposure to topics that are often difficult to grasp. As an example, the theme "From Past to Present" aligns with our exploration of the Revolutionary War in our social studies curriculum. The passages in this Close Read Guide include excerpts of famous speeches about the war, a short work of fiction on Paul Revere's ride, and an informational text on the role of children during the war. We can see evidence of the positive outcomes of this double-dosing: Our students' discussions and some of their essays combine what they've learned from social studies and from reading instruction. The chart on page 91 features a selection of grade-level studies that could coincide with social studies standards.

☆ **Consider criteria within the reading and other standards:** Most standards call for students to respond to literature in some manner. Incorporating this into your units enables students to employ knowledge of literary language, textual features and genres, among other standards-based skills.

Our reading standard emphasizes students' active engagement with literature. It also suggests that students read a variety of genres that extend beyond American culture to include world cultures. Our writing standards also support this call for more diverse literacy activities. In response, we created a themed unit called "Our Big World." The Close Read Guide for this unit includes two informational passages, one on traditional folklore and one on cultural clothing, and a tale about Anansi the trickster spider from African folklore.

☆ **Consider timely and high-interest topics:** If there are new, updated ideas that align with the topics of our curriculum, we might create a theme around these ideas so our guides reflect current events, ideas, and practices. We also keep track of high-interest topics even if the relationship to our curriculum is tangential. Some topics are too important to delay discussing, such as major events and situations that stir the nation, discoveries or new explorations in science, environmental breakthroughs, and so on. Kid-centric happenings—popular culture events, sport activities, and school-based issues including trends in the dietary regulation of school lunches—might also be suitable for a theme.

An easy way to track high-interest topics is to monitor children's magazines, TV programs, and age-appropriate documentaries for up-to-date, relevant offerings. These resources must appeal to students. Accessing topics identified through these resources can help you target your themes.

☆ **Consider what's happening at other grade levels:** It's unlikely that passages used in third grade would also be used in fourth grade, yet monitoring the themes used at other grade levels makes sense. In some instances it may be beneficial to build upon a previous topic, while in others, it is best to devise new themes. Sharing your thematic ideas with colleagues at different grade levels is usually all that's needed to determine your best course of action. Even when our thematic ideas are similar, we can easily make changes while retaining our planned selection of passages.

☆ **Select broad themes:** Using broad themes will give you the greatest flexibility as you make final decisions on the passages you want to include or exclude. A broader theme makes it easier for you to update and replace a passage with something that might be better suited to new or revised instructional objectives.

## Step 2: Compile the Mix of Passages

Once you've decided on a theme, you'll want to verify that your selection of passages represents a good mix of genres. As mentioned in Chapter 3, updates in the standards emphasize the use of a balance of informational and literary texts for students in grades K–6.

Many diverse text types fall within the broad categories of literature and informational text. For example, stories, dramas, and poetry are categories within literature, just as literary nonfiction, and historical, scientific, and technical texts are subgenres of informational text. (Review the guidelines on page 31 that describe the types of literature and informational texts.) Helping students recognize the nuances of a variety of text types and giving them occasions to practice applying and adapting their skills is too critical to leave to chance. Understanding a historical text takes a different set of skills than making sense of a scientific text. Students may strengthen their understanding of a complex passage by differentiating a chronological text structure from a cause-and-effect structure. Likewise, identifying the theme of a poem versus the theme of a myth may take a slightly different set of skills. Transferring skills among the variety of text types can be troublesome for students to master on their own. Your careful and purposeful mix of passages provides opportunities for students to practice and apply their skills.

# *Case Study:* Ask Arizona

One of the passages we included in our Accepting Ourselves and Others unit was "New Glasses: An All-New 'Look,'" from an advice column called "Ask Arizona." A letter writer expresses concerns about getting new glasses. Arizona responds by providing friendly advice and sharing an anecdote about a friend who had a similar experience. The passage also contains visuals, callouts, and captions. We selected this passage mostly because of its diverse content, features, and format. We anticipated that the unique and less-familiar advice-column format might be tricky for students and would thus be perfect for our close reading analysis. It also complemented the other passages in the guide and could pave the way for using more complicated passages, such as a "Letters to the Editor" column or even the historical letters that often appear in biographical works. This text presented different kinds of challenges that would help students build their skills.

## Step 3: Create Questions and Tasks

You will want to consider the quantity of questions and tasks you create as well as their mix and interaction. (A review of chapters 4 and 5 will help you produce text-dependent questions and tasks.) There is no hard rule for the number of items. Instead, we base this decision on the complexity of the passage, students' needs, and our judgment of how we can maximize the use of the text to constructively teach standards-based skills. We evaluate these criteria against the amount of time we feel each question and task will take. Our lessons can range from 15–45 minutes, so the amount of time we commit to them is an important consideration. To make the best use of time, students may complete tasks as morning work, during writing time, or as homework. They can tackle questions on their own, discuss them in shared pairs, and then with the whole class. We often use the third day for wrap-up activities. We'll complete and review all questions and tasks, and identify the theme or main idea of a passage.

## Step 4: Evaluate the Mix of Standards

It is essential to consider whether your Close Read Guide reflects a mix of standards. To ensure that we've covered all of the standards and emphasized the most challenging ones based on our students' needs, we track standards using an Instructional Unit Plan, which that is discussed on the next page.

Monitoring student performance during class discussions (as detailed in Chapter 6) and also as you work through a Close Read Guide provides a good indicator of which standards may be more challenging for students than others. By providing this type of formative data, the guides make student performance easy to track, enabling you to address your students' needs. For example, if a standard calls for students to identify the theme of a passage and to summarize key supporting details, are they able to demonstrate this skill in all genres of literature or is poetry tripping them up? Can they identify point of view in a variety of passages? Have you mindfully checked that point of view is covered well in one or more of your guides? As you compile your themed guides, make sure the standards are well represented.

## Step 5: Create a Culminating Activity

Wrap up the instructional unit by providing an outlet for students to demonstrate what they've learned about the critical ideas presented in the passages. Culminating activities also encourage a diverse use of standards. To end the Accepting Ourselves and Others close reading unit, students created a slideshow presentation for classmates on the theme of "All About Me." This activity encouraged students to use their writing skills, knowledge of technology, and speaking skills. We also asked them to incorporate ideas they have derived from the themes of the unit passages.

Many districts encourage the use of project-based learning. You can certainly integrate project-based learning into your Close Read Guide. Additionally, it lends itself well to engaging culminating activities and aligns well with standards-based research activities.

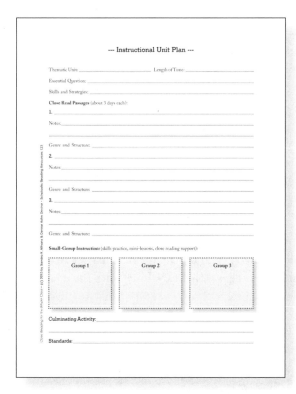

## Using an Instructional Unit Plan

A valuable procedure, especially as you monitor the mix of your passages, questions, tasks, and coverage of standards, is to plan your instructional units in advance. This will inform you as you compile your Close Read Guide and, once it is completed, provide an overview of key information about it. The Instructional Unit Plan includes the theme, an essential question, and the skills and strategies emphasized in the guide. Collectively, these three components comprise your instructional objectives. Do students understand how the passage reflects the theme and contributes to an understanding of the essential question? Can students demonstrate success with the skills and strategies emphasized in the guide? The plan also includes the title of each passage, a notes section (used to record tricky areas, unique features, links to earlier skill practice, ways to enhance instruction, and so on), and the genre and structure of each passage. The small-group instruction component helps you plan ways to support skills development for all of your students. Finally, the culminating activity is listed in the plan. A reproducible appears on page 123.

## Creating a Master Teacher Version and Student Guides

Once you've compiled a Close Read Guide for a theme, create a master teacher version that includes possible answers, teaching suggestions, and suggestions for connections among passages. Also create a Close Read Guide for each student so everyone can mark the passages, record answers to questions, and address tasks. Much of the supplemental notes included in our master teacher guide are based on shared experiences that we bring to our weekly planning meetings.

## Incorporating Tag-Alongs

Tag-alongs are close reading lessons that you can insert into an existing Close Read Guide. You can do this for a variety of reasons: The tag-along addresses a current and relevant issue, provides students with practice with a challenging skill, or is a newly published work that enhances your instructional objectives of the guide. Rather than excluding a passage (or waiting until you update your guide), you can embed these single-lesson close reads into the guide as tag-alongs. On page 92, you'll find a tag-along for *Nasreen's Secret School: A True Story from Afghanistan* (Winter, 2009), an illustrated informational book. We included this tag-along in our themed unit "Our Big World" because of its relevancy and cultural coverage.

## Using Teamwork to Create Close Read Guides

Teamwork enabled us to get to where we are today. A collaborative approach allowed us to divide and conquer the tasks in preparing Close Read Guides. This happened over time, as we gained comfort and skill with all stages of creating the guides, including selecting and ordering passages and devising questions and tasks. Although we are now beyond the start-up stage, we continue to work in teams to split up the workload in creating and revising guides. For example, all teachers search for reading materials using a variety of sources. Then we share the editing, keyboarding, and supplemental tasks such as checking against the standards. Most often, a team of two teachers tackles the job of researching technology-based tasks and a culminating activity. Although we meet weekly and briefly share our experiences in using the guides, we more formally review, discuss, and agree upon updates for them during superintendent conference days or over the summer. Changes are then made to the database, and a master copy of the student Close Read Guide and the master teacher guide are made available to each teacher through an electronic database.

### *Electronic Storage and Retrieval*

Storing materials electronically allows you to quickly and easily change and update them. It may be necessary for you to scan the passages into an electronic document or re-key them if there are issues with the quality. We have also doctored some passages by adding illustrations or photographs to the text. (Make sure your school media specialist has permission or the proper licenses to use materials in this manner. Materials in the public domain may be used flexibly.)

## Rubric Assessment and Student Feedback

Although Close Read Guides are used primarily for guided instruction, they can also be used for formal and informal assessment. In today's classrooms, teachers are held accountable for student performance. Additionally, most districts require teachers to provide instruction that is informed by data. This means that

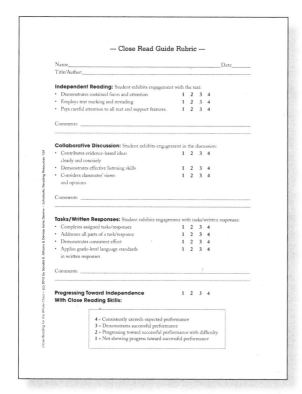

ongoing review and analysis of student performance is a must. Most teachers use formal and informal assessments to do this. As students will be working through a Close Read Guide for several weeks, you may wish to monitor their performance, formally or informally, using a rubric similar to the one on page 124.

This rubric evaluates student performance across four areas: (1) independent reading, (2) collaborative discussion, tasks, and/or (3) tasks and/or written responses to questions, and written responses to questions, and (4) the degree to which students are progressing toward independence with close reading skills. This rubric uses a numeric scale from 1–4 to evaluate student performance, which corresponds to the grading systems used on our district's report cards. You can also use this rubric to provide summative feedback to students at the conclusion of a unit.

## Student Self-Evaluation

Another way we monitor student progress is through a self-evaluation questionnaire on the inside front cover of each guide. These evaluations address specific skills that are emphasized in the guide. A copy of an evaluation appears on page 88. Here, we ask students to gauge their success in understanding evidence, responding to questions and tasks, and recognizing theme (which was emphasized in this guide). We also encourage students to reflect on areas they found difficult or easy. Students complete this evaluation at the end of a unit, and we often share their responses during our team meetings so we can make changes to the guide or address a student's needs in other ways, such as through small-group instruction.

## One Size Does Not Fit All: Flexibility for Teachers

A final benefit to using Close Read Guides is that you can use them flexibly in your classroom. You can tailor your instruction by emphasizing questions and tasks that contain skills your students are struggling with and need to practice. Likewise, you can put less emphasis on, or skip over, materials that reinforce skills students have already mastered. Class discussion time is another area that can be treated flexibly. Although close reading discussions are based on the questions and tasks in a guide, you can steer discussions in a direction that aids students more effectively.

You can also adapt guides to suit your teaching style. For example, some teachers may choose to use text-dependent questions primarily for whole-class discussion, while others may prefer that students respond in writing to questions following whole-class discussion. Some teachers may collect and review students' guides daily, while others may review them after a passage is completed. Some teachers may swap out a story with a tag-along, and others may use the passages in the guide as they are.

## Changing Over Time

Since creating our first batch of Close Read Guides, we have replaced some passages, tweaked some questions, and modified some tasks. Everyone in education today recognizes that seeking improvement, embracing the changes that foster it, and accommodating the changes swiftly is the new way to operate. Change is simply the outcome that makes learning an ongoing process.

## *Five Tips* for Creating Close Read Guides

1.  **Stay focused and don't stray from your goals and objectives**. A new undertaking can be overwhelming. It's important to stay focused and move at a steady pace through the steps for creating a Close Read Guide. Be on the lookout for things that use up your time, such as getting sidetracked in good but unproductive discussions. Mulling over your ideas and plans too much may cause you to reach a point of diminishing returns. Reserve the right to go back and make changes, but while creating your guides, keep moving forward.

2.  **Mix up passages.** The passages you select for your guide will all share a common theme, but this doesn't mean they should be redundant or repetitive. With a good, diverse mix of passages, you can expand and enrich students' views, which may be narrow or oversimplified, especially on common themes. Look for a range of passages that can deliver an assortment of experiences. Remember that your first impression of the value of a passage may not be reliable (which is why the 5S Teacher Read is so important). This is a noteworthy caution as you compile your mix of passages as well. Consider how a passage contributes to your mix.

3.  **Mix it up more.** Your questions, tasks, and discussions should also interact in ways that offer variety. There is no need to repeat questions and tasks as you move from passage to passage. Also, forcing skills practice with a passage that doesn't contain a good application of those skills is like trying to force water from a stone—it simply won't work!

4.  **Allow flexibility with your timing.** As you calculate the amount of time it may take to read, discuss, and address questions and tasks for the passages in a guide, recognize that in practice your timing may be very different. It's critical to be flexible, but keep some parameters. Base your pacing on your professional judgment and determine how much time you are willing to devote to a passage, not necessarily on how much time it will take. You will base this distinction on your knowledge of your students' needs and the degree to which a passage meets them.

5.  **Don't reinvent the wheel year after year.** Creating a Close Read Guide is an investment of time that you must maximize. Whenever possible, consider how you can upgrade your guide as opposed to starting from scratch. You will want to adjust your instruction as students become more skilled with the standards and with close reading strategies. Also, you will want the subject matter in your passages to remain current and timely. Subtle changes can be made quickly and easily by introducing them through your discussions. Your guide may not need changes. Other times, you may need to make major changes, such as swapping out a passage or two. When this occurs, you still can use your experience and knowledge with selecting passages and crafting questions and tasks more efficiently. Don't underestimate the value of this practical know-how! Use it to your advantage.

## Professional Development Activities

Using the guidelines in this chapter, brainstorm six themes for effective and engaging Close Read Guides. Discuss ways in which your themes align with your grade-level standards and curriculum. Number your themes in a sequential order based on criteria you establish (e.g., how your Close Read Guides might align with science or social studies instruction or subject matter complexity). You may also want to devise essential questions that coordinate well with your themes.

Select one theme from the list you brainstormed in the first activity. Using that theme, begin the process for making a Close Read Guide. First, list the mix of passages you might like to feature. Your list could include how you might mix passages and also how you might mix questions and tasks. Next, brainstorm a culminating activity that aligns with the theme and identify the standards students would likely use to complete it.

Review the Close Read Guide Rubric on page 124. Discuss with colleagues how you might use this rubric with your students. Consider how to adjust or refine this rubric so it becomes your own.

## Inside Front Cover

## Greetings!

This packet contains several reading passages that we'll be examining very carefully. We call these "close reads," and although some parts may be challenging—have no fear! We'll work through them together and answer questions using evidence from the passages. You'll also find some great tasks to do, which will help you gain a deeper understanding of the passages. Enjoy!

## Self-Evaluation

**Please complete at the end of this unit.** Tell us how you think you did in this unit by checking the box that best describes your experience with these reading passages.

1. I understand how to use "evidence" in a passage to answer questions/tasks.
   ☐ Not Really  ☐ Sometimes  ☐ Always

2. The questions/tasks helped me gain a deeper understanding of the passage.
   ☐ Not Really  ☐ Sometimes  ☐ Always

3. I understand what a "theme" is and could describe it for each passage.
   ☐ Not Really  ☐ Sometimes  ☐ Always

4. The hardest thing for me in this unit was _____

5. The easiest thing for me in this unit was _____

_____

_____

## Front Cover

_____ 's Close Read Guide

*How do our feelings about ourselves affect us and others?*

**Essential Question:**
Often linked to theme, it helps focus instruction and provides a broad context for learning.

**Self Portrait:**
Students draw a picture of themselves in response to their reading. It's completed at the end of unit to encourage reflection on theme.

## SELF PoRTRAIT

Theme: Accepting Ourselves and Others

**Passages:**
A guide typically includes three to four passages. "The Champion of Quiet" is a short story; the other two passages are informational articles.

## READING SELECTIONS:

"The Champion of Quiet"
"Deaf and Blind—Not Dumb!"
"New Glasses: An All-New 'Look'"

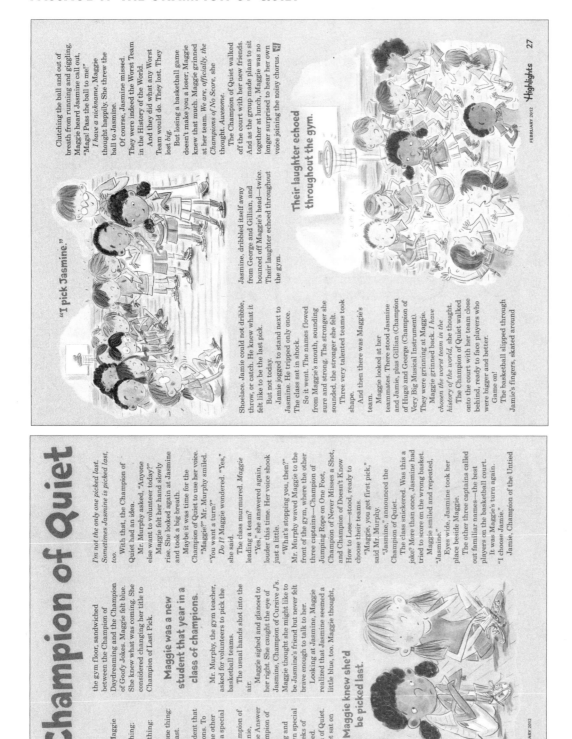

# The Champion of Quiet

By Tracy Stewart
Art by Paula Becker

It was a Tuesday, and Maggie hated Tuesdays.

Tuesdays meant one thing: gym class.

Gym class meant one thing: picking teams.

Picking teams meant one thing: Maggie would be picked last. As always.

Maggie was a new student that year in a class of champions. To help herself remember the other kids, she'd come up with a special title for each one.

There was Kevin, Champion of the Clean Desk; and Lynnie, Champion of Knowing the Answer First; and Caroline, Champion of Tardy. And so on.

She'd had to think long and hard to figure out her own special title. After five whole weeks of school, Maggie had decided. She was the Champion of Quiet. The Champion of Quiet sat on the gym floor, sandwiched between the Champion of Daydreaming and the Champion of Goofy Jokes. Maggie felt blue. She knew what was coming. She considered changing her title to Champion of Last Pick.

### Maggie was a new student that year in a class of champions.

Mr. Murphy, the gym teacher, asked for volunteers to pick the basketball teams.

The usual hands shot into the air.

Maggie sighed and glanced to her right. She caught the eye of Jasmine, Champion of Cursive J's. Maggie thought she might like to be Jasmine's friend but never felt brave enough to talk to her.

Looking at Jasmine, Maggie realized that Jasmine seemed a little blue, too. Maggie thought,

### Maggie knew she'd be picked last.

*I'm not the only one picked last. Sometimes Jasmine is picked last, too.*

With that, the Champion of Quiet had an idea.

Mr. Murphy asked, "Anyone else want to volunteer today?"

Maggie felt her hand slowly rise. She looked again at Jasmine and took a big breath.

Maybe it was time for the Champion of Quiet to use her voice.

"Maggie?" Mr. Murphy smiled. "You want a turn?"

*Do I?* Maggie wondered. "Yes," she said.

The class murmured. *Maggie leading a team?*

"Yes," she answered again, louder this time. Her voice shook just a little.

"What's stopping you, then?" Mr. Murphy waved Maggie to the front of the gym, where the other three captains—Champion of Jumping Rope on One Foot, Champion of Never Misses a Shot, and Champion of Doesn't Know How to Lose—stood, ready to choose their teams.

"Maggie, you get first pick," said Mr. Murphy.

"Jasmine," announced the Champion of Quiet.

The class snickered. Was this a joke? More than once, Jasmine had tried to score on the wrong basket.

Maggie smiled and repeated, "Jasmine."

Eyes wide, Jasmine took her place beside Maggie.

The other three captains called out familiar names—the best players on the basketball court.

It was Maggie's turn again.

"I choose Jamie."

Jamie, Champion of the Untied Shoelace. Jamie could not dribble, throw, or catch. He knew what it felt like to be the last pick.

But not today.

Jamie jogged to stand next to Jasmine. He tripped only once. The class sat in shock.

So it went. The names flowed from Maggie's mouth, sounding sure and strong. The stronger she sounded, the stronger she felt.

Three very talented teams took shape.

And then there was Maggie's team.

Maggie looked at her teammates. There stood Jasmine and Jamie, plus Gillian (Champion of Hugs) and George (Champion of Very Big Musical Instrument).

They were grinning at Maggie.

Maggie grinned back. *I have chosen the worst team in the history of the world,* she thought.

The Champion of Quiet walked onto the court with her team close behind, ready to face players who were bigger and better.

Game on!

The basketball slipped through Jamie's fingers, skated around and out of breath from running and giggling, Maggie heard Jasmine call out, "Mags! Pass the ball to me!"

*I have a nickname,* Maggie thought happily. She threw the ball to Jasmine.

Of course, Jasmine missed. They were indeed the Worst Team in the History of the World.

And they did what any Worst Team would do. They lost. They lost *big.*

But losing a basketball game doesn't make you a loser. Maggie knew that much. Maggie grinned at her team. *We are, officially, the Champions of No Score,* she thought. *Awesome.*

The Champion of Quiet walked off the court with her new friends. And as the group made plans to sit together at lunch, Maggie was no longer surprised to hear her own voice joining the noisy chorus.

**"I pick Jasmine."**

**Their laughter echoed throughout the gym.**

Jasmine, dribbled itself away from George and Gillian, and bounced off Maggie's head—twice. Their laughter echoed throughout the gym.

26 Highlights FEBRUARY 2012

Highlights FEBRUARY 2012 27

# QUESTIONS, TASKS, AND ACTIVITIES FOR "THE CHAMPION OF QUIET"

T1. Complete a Bubble Map featuring Maggie's character traits. Then select one trait from your map and provide evidence from the passage to show how Maggie demonstrates this trait.

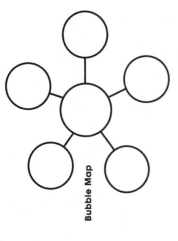

**Bubble Map**

The character trait from my Bubble Map is _____

In the story, Maggie shows this trait when _____

T2. On a separate sheet of paper, describe how Maggie changes from the beginning of the story to the end. Be sure to use text evidence to support your answer. Include the following:
- Describe what Maggie is like at the beginning of the story.
- Explain what causes her to change.
- Describe what Maggie is like at the end of the story.

**Day 3 Wrap-up Activities:**
1. Teacher briefly reviews the discussion about the end of page 27 and completed tasks.
2. Teacher encourages discussion of theme of entire passage. Students record theme.

The theme of this passage is _____

---

## --- Close Read Student Guide ---
### Unit 1: Accepting Ourselves and Others

**Title:** "The Champion of Quiet"          **Length of**
**Time:** 3 days
**Author:** Tracy Stewart

**Day 1 Activities:**
- Teacher introduces passage. Students read pages 26 and 27 STOP independently.
- Teacher reads pages 26 and 27 STOP aloud. Students follow along.
- Teacher asks guiding questions and assigns tasks for pages 26 and 27 STOP of the passage.

**Discussion Questions and Tasks**
Q1. What is Maggie's problem with Tuesdays? Use evidence from the passage.
Q2. What does the author convey in the sentences "Maggie felt blue" and "Jasmine seemed a little blue, too"? Use evidence from the passage to support your answer.
Q3. Why does Maggie nickname everyone "champion of" something? Explain whether she is being mean.

T1. In your own words, explain what Maggie means when she says, "Maybe it was time for the Champion of Quiet to use her voice." Use evidence from the passage to support your answer.

T2. Use a paint strip to craft a list of synonyms for the word *blue*.

**Day 2 Activities:**
- Teacher briefly reviews discussions about pages 26 and 27 STOP and tasks students completed.
- Teacher introduces end of page 27 and students read end of page independently.
- Teacher reads end of page 27 aloud as students follow along.
- Teacher asks guiding questions and assigns tasks for end of page 27.

**Discussion Questions and Tasks**
Q1. Why are some words or phrases printed in an italic font?
Q2. What important event is a turning point for Maggie?
Q3. Near the end of the story, Jasmine calls Maggie "Mags." Why did this make Maggie happy? Use evidence from the story to support your answer.

## A Selection of Themes in the Social Studies Framework

| Grade 2 My Community and Other Communities | Grade 3 Communities Around the World | Grade 4 New York State and Local History and Government | Grade 5 The Western Hemisphere | Grade 6 The Eastern Hemisphere |
|---|---|---|---|---|
| 2.1. A community is a population of various individuals in a common location. | 3.1. Geographic regions have unifying characteristics and can be studied using a variety of tools. | 4.1. Geography of New York State | 5.1. Early Peoples of the Americas | 6.1. Present-Day Eastern Hemisphere Geography |
| 2.2. People share similarities and differences with others in their own community and with other communities. | 3.2. The location of world communities can be described using geographic tools and vocabulary. | 4.2. Native American Groups and the Environment | 5.2. Complex Societies and Civilizations | 6.2. The First Humans Through the Neolithic Revolution in the Eastern Hemisphere |
| 2.3. The United States is founded on the principles of democracy, and these principles are reflected in all types of communities. | 3.3. Geographic factors often influence where people settle and form communities. | 4.3. Colonial and Revolutionary Period in New York | 5.3. European Exploration and Its Effects | 6.3. Early River Valley Civilizations in the Eastern Hemisphere |
| 2.4. Communities have rules and laws that affect how they function. | 3.4. Each community or culture has a unique history, including heroic figures, traditions, and holidays. | 4.4. Government | 5.4. Geography of the Western Hemisphere | 6.4. Comparative World Religions (ca. 2000 B.C.E.– ca. 630 C.E.) |
| 2.5. Geography and natural resources shape where and how urban, suburban, and rural communities develop and how they sustain themselves. | 3.5. Communities across the world share cultural similarities and differences. | 4.5. In Search of Freedom and a Call for Change | 5.5. Comparative Cultures | 6.5. Comparative Classical Civilizations in the Eastern Hemisphere (ca. 600 B.C.E.– ca. 500 C.E.) |
| 2.6. Identifying continuities and changes over time can help us understand historical developments. | 3.6. Communities from around the world interact with other people and communities and exchange cultural ideas and practices. | 4.6. Westward Movement and Industrialization | 5.6. Government | 6.6. Mediterranean World: Feudal Western Europe, the Byzantine Empire, and the Islamic Caliphates (ca. 600 C.E.–ca. 1450) |

# Close Read Teacher Guide
## Unit 2 Tag-Along Picture Book: Our Big World

**Title: Nasreen's Secret School**                           **Amount of Time: 1–2 days**
**Author: Jeanette Winter**

. . . . . . . . . . . . . . . . . . . . . . . . . . . . . . . . . . . . . . . . . . . . . . . . . . . . . . . . . . . . . . . . . . . . . . . . . . . .

**Pre-reading:** Review of world map to highlight Afghanistan, discussion of cultural names
(e.g., "Nasreen" in the title)

**Page 1 (Q1)** *Based on your reading of the Author's Note, explain who wrote this book and why.*
*Summarize the key ideas in the note.* (Students should extract that the author is contrasting
women's rights, privileges, and freedoms before and after the Taliban takeover. Teachers may
want to point out the structure of the bulleted list to highlight this information. Students must
clearly grasp the differences in their summary.)

**Page 5 (Q2)** *Who is telling this story?* (Students may need some help clarifying that the
grandmother is telling the story. Throughout the work, this is sometimes confusing.)

**Pages 6–7 (Q3)** *Who causes a major change?* (Although the text does not go into great detail
about the Taliban, students can glean that "soldiers" who are part of the Taliban create
tremendous change. Where art and music once flourished, they are now gone. Also, girls are no
longer able to attend school as they had been for the past two generations.)

**Pages 8–9 (Q4)** *What inferences can you make about this situation when you compare it to*
*what could happen in the United States?* (Students may need some help grasping that these
developments would likely not take place in the United States where people's rights are
protected. Only under special circumstances are authorities able to enter a person's home
uninvited and take someone into custody against his or her will. Clearly, there is a difference.
It may also be necessary to clarify that Nasreen's father was taken away.)

# Chapter 8

## Nitty-Gritty Strategies and Take-5 Mini-Lessons for Close Reading

One of the most beneficial ways to strengthen students' close reading skills is to provide them with strategies that bolster their comprehension of complex texts. In this chapter we share a collection of basic, no-frills strategies that support text analysis and help guide students to deeper-level understandings. We also include sample Take-5 Mini-Lessons for some of the strategies we introduced in Chapter 2.

## Take-5 Mini-Lesson Protocol

We introduce strategies to our students in a streamlined manner, with a Take-5 Mini-Lesson directly preceding our close reading lesson. The mini-lesson covers the basics of one strategy only, and we strive to limit lessons to 5 minutes so we can move right into close reading. Once we begin, we provide further instruction in the use of that new strategy in the authentic context of the close reading lesson. We model its application and monitor how effectively students are applying it.

Here's how this works: As you'll recall, our close reading protocol includes independent student reading, a teacher read-aloud, and then discussion of questions and tasks. Our Take-5 Mini-Lesson exists outside of the actual close reading lesson, as if we've taken a short break. But we immediately resume our plans and embed our strategy instruction into the context of the lesson. We've found that students gain proficiency with a skill through repeated, authentic practice with a variety of text types. Returning to our planned close reading lesson immediately after introducing the strategy reflects our priority of productively spending our reading time doing just that: reading effectively and strategically, even as we are learning how to apply new strategies.

Delivery of the mini-lesson needs to be as streamlined as its content. Your mini-lesson will reflect your instructional style, but it's essential that you keep it short, concise, and mostly teacher directed. There will be time for interaction later in the close reading lesson and/or during additional support instruction, if necessary, to compensate for the brevity of the mini-lesson.

## An Overview of the Strategies

We organize these nitty-gritty close reading strategies into three groups:

- Golden Group of Strategies
- Strategies for New Areas of Emphasis
- Traditional Strategy Instruction

# Golden Group of Strategies

These strategies, introduced in Chapter 2, support the development of deep reading skills that are essential to close reading. They are often interconnected and can be used in combination with the other strategies described in this chapter. They include the following:

- Text marking
- Launching jump-start clues
- Listening to my inner voice
- Pursuing evidence
- Allowing the passage to speak for itself

## Text Marking

When students mark a passage by coding it while reading, they are identifying elements such as rich content vocabulary, critical ideas, significant phrases, and other noteworthy details. Students may also mark text by annotating the gist of the meaning in a margin, which is usually performed for larger chunks of text such as paragraphs, stanzas, or text under subheadings.

There are many benefits to text marking, including the following:

- **It encourages students' active engagement with the text.** Text marking requires readers to be alert, thinking about what to mark in a passage, and how to mark it, as they read. This process combats passive, disengaged reading.
- **It prompts students to look for and detect critical features in a passage.** Students move systematically through a text and identify key features that will help them make sense of their reading.
- **It helps students detect the structure of a passage.** This awareness also supports their understanding of key ideas and details.
- **It helps students slow down and think through deeper-level meaning.** Preparing gist statements often helps students gain a greater understanding of a text, extending beyond the shallow understanding that a cursory reading provides.
- **It encourages a deeper-level awareness of texts.** Students quickly become able to recognize the nuances of diverse genres, as well as to uncover the unique features of an author's style of writing. Both help students gain an appreciation for the craft of writing.
- **It serves as a valuable place marker.** Students know where to return to in the passage to reread, pull evidence, or square their ideas with the text.

Text marking isn't a skill that requires a rigid precision. The marked-up passages of two grade-level readers who receive the same instruction in this strategy will likely have much in common as well as some differences. This is completely acceptable and is actually to be expected.

Gauging whether students have detected key ideas, critical structural elements, content-rich vocabulary, and other key features in the text is one way to monitor the effectiveness of their text marking. If a student seems to be marking too much of a passage at the expense of reading for meaning, you might want to investigate their use of the skill more thoroughly. Some students truly benefit from marking a lot of text, while others may not recognize they are misusing the strategy. Likewise, too little text marking could indicate that a student is reading too quickly. This, too, will require further investigation.

In addition to monitoring students' text-marking activities, you'll also want to read the gist statements they've written in the margins to determine if they have grasped the essence of the text. Both forms of text marking should be treated as one indicator that must be considered alongside others, such as the level of comprehension they demonstrate while participating in discussions, responding to questions, and completing tasks. Guidelines for building students' text-marking skills appears on page 107. A Take-5 Mini-Lesson to introduce text marking begins on page 108.

## Launching Jump-Start Clues

Students perform this pre-reading skill as a way to become engaged with the text. They leap into making meaning immediately, skimming and scanning the passage and looking for quick clues that help inform their ideas about the genre, content, structure, and other pertinent aspects of the text. For example, students might scan a passage and notice it has numerous subheadings, a couple of charts, and a sidebar with a labeled diagram. They might also skim over the title, "Experts Question 'Eco-Friendly' Cleansers," and get a vague sense of the content. From this brief exploration, they might suspect this is an informational article of a scientific nature about green cleansers. Based on their growing knowledge of informational texts, their expectations trigger questions and a call to action; they'll not only dig for the main idea and purpose of the passage, but they'll also pursue whether the author is credible and if the claims and findings he or she presents are valid.

Students know that their pre-reading ideas are apt to change. Still, launching jump-start clues serves the purpose of building preliminary knowledge and expectations that are either confirmed or reshaped as students read. Teachers no longer provide students with many pre-reading scaffolds, yet teaching them to come up with feasible ideas on their own encourages independence. One way to determine if students are able to correctly identify a genre is to have them note or code this alongside the title before they start their independent reading, for example, using an "I" for informational texts and an "L" for literature. They can then identify and code the specific genre: "P" for poetry, "B" for biography, "AB" for autobiography, and so on. There are many different ways you can instruct students to code a passage, but keep your system simple and easy to apply.

As a final note, although this skill is one that can help students early on, gaining proficiency with it happens over time as they build their knowledge and experience. They need to work with a variety of text types and genres to build diverse skills. Based on your assessment, you may find that you need to provide mini-lessons in which you integrate genre and text structure. You can then display anchor charts to help students learn to distinguish one genre from another and to then set expectations. A selection of these expectations appears in the Identifying Text Structures discussion beginning on page 99. Should students not grasp genre and structure clues after you've provided lessons and practiced routinely, you will want to offer additional small-group instruction on this outside of your close reading class time.

With this pre-reading process, students set baseline expectations (a purpose and a path for reading) and activate prior knowledge (to guide them along the path). Students recognize they may make adjustments to their fluid thinking through ongoing self-monitoring. A Take-5 Mini-Lesson on launching jump-start clues begins on page 111, and a reproducible for students to use as they learn how to use these clues appears on page 125.

## Listening to My Inner Voice

A student's ability to listen to his or her inner voice, or to have "in-the-head conversations" (a term used by Laura Robb) is critical. As students start to build awareness of how new standards-based skills can help them with comprehension, model how they can listen to their inner dialogue as they apply all the strategies in this chapter. For example, students might use the prompts on the Jump-Start Clues Checklist to guide their inner dialogue as they speculate about genre. Eventually, they will internalize these prompts and learn to talk though their ideas (in their head).

As the chart below shows, students can build and strengthen their independent close reading skills by probing a passage and monitoring their understanding. The first-, second-, and third-level probes help them identify the genre, activate background knowledge, and set expectations for reading. These probes use the jump-start strategy and rely on students' grade-level knowledge of literary basics. The fourth- and

## Probing a Passage Checklist

| | |
|---|---|
| **First-Level Probe**<br>• Is the passage literature or informational? | **Jump-Start Strategy** |
| **Second-Level Probe**<br>• Can I distinguish a particular genre within those broad categories? | **Jump-Start Strategy** |
| **Third-Level Probe**<br>• What are my expectations based on my knowledge of genre?<br>• What are my expectations based on my knowledge of text structure?<br>• What are my other expectations based on my prior knowledge and experience? | **Necessary Background Knowledge to BridgeJump-Start Strategy and Monitoring***<br>*\* Ensure that students are provided with grade-level appropriate knowledge in genre, text structure, and craft literary basics.* |
| **Fourth-Level Probe**<br>• As I begin to read, I'm able to build understanding of the passage. I believe my expectations are on track so far.<br>OR<br>• As I begin to read, I'm having trouble understanding the passage. I need to adjust my initial thinking and expectations. | **Student Monitoring**<br>Students determine if their expectations and preliminary understanding of the text align. If they do, students continue moving forward. If not, they adjust their expectations. |
| **Fifth-Level Probe**<br>• I'm on track to build cohesive understanding. | **Ongoing Student Monitoring**<br>Students continue to monitor meaning against expectations, adjusting and shaping as necessary. |

fifth-level probes validate students' interpretation of the text from start to finish. These probes rely on students' ongoing monitoring.

Questions prompt the dialogue process. Modeling this type of inner dialogue may be necessary for many of the strategies featured in this chapter. You can easily integrate modeling into your planned close reading instruction. A Take-5 Mini-Lesson on listening to inner voice begins on page 113.

## Pursuing Evidence

In order for our students to become skilled at identifying and locating evidence, we must build up their skills through text-based questions and tasks. We also want to help students internalize the process of validating their thinking as they build meaning so they can become critical readers. You can initiate direct instruction of these skills beginning with your first mini-lesson in which you introduce close reading (see page 23). Then continue to develop students' skills and proficiency across text types and genres. Here are several key points to consider:

☆ **Defining what evidence is:** Students may need direct instruction in the true meaning of the term *evidence*. Even though their standards-based instruction at earlier grade levels has undoubtedly provided them with a working understanding of the term, there may be nuances at your grade level that are unfamiliar. For example, some students may not be familiar with the idea of weighing multiple pieces of evidence to determine which is strongest. Having a preliminary discussion to define evidence and sharing ways in which students can use it while reading will help you to ensure that everyone is on the same page.

☆ **Locating varied forms of evidence:** Making use of all the information in a passage might be something that needs emphasis. For example, students may not think to use information that appears in captions or sidebars as evidence. Also, they might not have as much experience and ease in using numerical data from a table or chart as evidence as they do with print. Providing opportunities to build on the skills that may be lacking is essential. Integrating science and social studies lessons into your close reading instruction offers a good avenue to do this. You can easily make this a priority as you create text-based questions for a passage.

☆ **Building evidence for inferences:** Helping students support their inferences by using clues in the text can be challenging. When an author doesn't include explicit evidence, students must delve into their own thinking and determine what caused them to arrive at an understanding. More complex works of literature, even readers theater or other forms of drama, provide good opportunities for students to build this skill. However, working with informational text is also important and relies on a different set of skills. For example, seeking out action-based clues to explain a character's feelings is a typical type of inference that students must support while reading literature. While reading informational text, they often need to infer an author's views based on the manner in which ideas are presented. Here, students might need to look at structural elements, such as the weight an author gives to certain matters. Word choice is another factor that helps students develop insights into an author's views. The different forms evidence may take in literature and informational text is something to briefly highlight during your close reading discussion time when there is an authentic opportunity to do so.

☆ **Analyzing an author's use of evidence:** As students work with informational text, they must be taught how to analyze an author's use of evidence and how to match evidence to the points he or she makes.

☆ **Gauging the weight of evidence and ranking it:** All evidence is not created equal, and students must grasp this point. What makes one piece of evidence stronger than another can be tricky to define. One piece of evidence may be stronger than another in one instance but weaker in a second instance. For example, students might use data to support their response to a question that calls for a comparison between the earth's distance to the sun and to the moon. Here, using quantitative data that appears in the passage may be the best evidence. However, this doesn't mean that data is always the stronger form of evidence to use. The relevancy of one piece of support against another depends on the context.

⭐ **Detecting a lack of reliable evidence:** Searching for something that's not there is another avenue of evidence hunting that requires practice. Sometimes, the absence of information speaks loudly. This is true in literature as well as in informational text. We've all experienced this when we've wondered why a character suddenly acts in an unexpected manner. We learn as the plot unfolds that the author deliberately included this event to contribute to our understanding at a later time. We've also questioned why an author didn't include statistical information about a vital element in a nonfiction article. This lack of evidence often helps us determine whether an author has reliably presented all the information that will help us evaluate an argument or claim. Our ability to question these missing pieces helps us make meaning and/or make use of information in meaningful ways. Students may not grasp this notion, especially struggling students who cannot rely on their questions to serve these purposes. Their difficulty in making meaning may overwhelm their ability to distinguish helpful, guiding questions. Continuing to model this process and also encouraging peer discussion is a helpful way to scaffold this skill.

Based on your students' knowledge and experience, you might want to start with (or review) basic evidence-seeking strategies before moving them toward some of the more complex strategies discussed above. To practice strategies, we encourage our students to return to the passage and text-mark their support evidence. We might also have them note the text-based question they're answering alongside the evidence, for example, coding their evidence with "Q1" to designate a response to Question 1, and so on. This allows us to see students' thought processes. As they progress in developing this skill, we have them assign a numerical value to their marked evidence to identify which is strongest. We've found that students get a handle on these strategies best through repeated hands-on practice with a variety of text types and genres. Exposing students to rich and varied materials is critical. See the Take-5 Mini-Lesson on locating and using text evidence that begins on page 115.

## Allowing the Passage to Speak for Itself

We want our students to understand that their skills interact in unique ways as they read a passage. This is because each passage they encounter is unique. Students cannot anticipate which skills will be most helpful to them until they "allow the passage to speak for itself." This is especially relevant during test-taking situations, when the purpose for reading is to demonstrate students' comprehension skills. Students may not know what type of passage they will encounter in these situations. It is therefore critical that they remain open to using any and all of their strategies based on what they find in the text. As an example, to understand the main idea of a text, readers might need to call upon a variety of skills, such as gauging the emphasis an author has placed on ideas. To understand poetry, readers need to be skilled in understanding figurative language such as metaphors and similes. To understand historical texts, readers need to be able to recognize cause-and-effect relationships. We stress this point with students to emphasize the importance of the analytical part of reading, versus just reading words.

The jump-start strategy helps initiate this process of reading a variety of rich texts in diverse genres. Developing it involves building students' knowledge and experience with the other standards-based skills. You can help support this kind of mastery by searching out interesting reading materials of all kinds: passages with unique structural formats, for example, or texts that include unpredictable elements. You can familiarize your students with these tricky elements by building them into your questions and discussions, and you can ask students in a culminating activity to explain how the author supported the main idea or theme of the passage.

# Strategies for New Areas of Emphasis

In keeping with the times, readers must now pay heightened attention to text structure, point of view, and author intentions. All represent viable pathways for students to extract meaning from a passage. Largely underutilized in the past, these areas are emphasized in today's standards and encourage students to expand the way they explore texts. The strategies in this grouping help students filter information from a passage by doing the following:

- Identifying text structure
- Recognizing point of view
- Recognizing author intentions

Suggestions for mini-lessons appear below and can easily be adapted to fit into the format of the Take-5 Mini-Lesson. As you'll note, these lessons can vary in length depending upon student background knowledge, the complexity of the grade-level standard, the passage, and how you chose to weave your instruction together.

## Identifying Text Structures

Students need a solid understanding of text structure including the ones listed at right.

Identifying text structure helps students become stronger readers. First and foremost, it makes them aware that good texts present ideas in structured ways, not randomly. Students also may be unaware that certain types of texts, such as biographies, are typically organized chronologically, or that most fiction begins with a problem and ends with a resolution.

| Literature | Informational |
| --- | --- |
| • Stories | • Recognition of Text Features |
| • Dramas | • Chronology |
| • Poems | • Comparison |
| | • Cause/Effect |
| | • Problem/Solution |

Once students can recognize the structure of a passage, it helps them set expectations for their reading (which they can then monitor), enables them to connect ideas and build cohesive understanding, and guides them as they square their thinking against the author's intention. Knowing how to detect and make use of text structure aids students' deep-level reading and enhances their ability to understand complex texts. The three mini-lessons that follow help support students' understanding of text structures.

### Mini-Lesson 1: Linking Text Structures to Genres

Guide students to take note of structural elements as you work through texts in various genres. For example, as they read a biography about a well-known person, they will note that it is organized chronologically or in time sequence; these types of texts often begin with the individual's birth, move through his or her childhood, and then cover adulthood. Students may also notice that photographs are often included that follow this structure. Record these observations on a biography anchor chart. (We refer to this as a "blended anchor chart" because it includes structural information in addition to a definition.) Over time, students will associate this structural pattern with biographies. They will also expect to see certain features with this genre, such as photographs. You might want to make and display other blended anchor charts as you introduce new genres.

As students build their background knowledge with diverse works of literature and informational texts, they will easily be able to grasp how to turn their knowledge into expectations. These expectations can then be used to guide, monitor, and square their understanding.

We launch our text structure mini-lessons with the familiar genres of realistic fiction and biography. Here is a selection of text-marking codes that you can add to your anchor charts:

**Literature**

Realistic Fiction (RF)
Mythology (Myth)
Poetry (P)
Drama (D)

**Informational**

Biography (B)
General Informational (I)
Historical Informational (HI)
Scientific Informational (SI)

Students can provide ideas for coding other blended genre anchor charts you introduce. Keeping your system simple is key. You can combine related items on a single chart. For example, historical documents, such as speeches, broadsides, illustrations, and paintings, might go under the heading "Historical Informational" with mild differences specified by a star or another symbol.

## *Mini-Lesson 2:* **Look for Trigger Words**

Teaching trigger words that signal associations between ideas is another way to help students use text structures and build comprehension. Common text structures often use trigger words and phrases such as those shown in the chart below.

### Chronological Text Structure

*before • at first • in the beginning • next • step 1, 2, 3*
*then • afterward • shortly thereafter • finally • date sequence*
*last • in the end • first, second, third • moments later • time sequence*
A chronological structure tells us that information, events, or ideas are presented in an order.

### Comparison Text Structure

*same • similar • both • share • alike*
*however • yet • different • while • on the other hand*
A comparison structure tells us how information, events, things, or ideas are similar
to or different from other information, events, things or ideas.

### Cause-and-Effect Text Structure

*since • because • as a result • therefore • due to • thus*
*hence • in turn • consequently • given that • then • so*
A cause-and-effect structure tells us that there is a relationship between events, ideas, or occurrences.
Something happens first (the cause), which results in something else happening (the effect).

### Problem/Solution Text Structure

*problem • issue • situation • matter • dispute • argument • conflict*
*solution • result • resolution • ending • agreement • plan of action • resolve*
A problem/solution structure tells us the information is presented as a problem that is then solved.

When you encounter these triggers from your mini-lessons during close reading instruction, instruct students to draw a box around them as a way to make these words stand out from the other words in the passage. This may help some students comprehend complex historical or biographical texts; by scanning the dates, they can better grasp the sequence of connected events. Likewise, drawing a box around a list of steps in a scientific experiment or a set of procedures helps students understand that the order of information in the text is critical and recognize that order. Students might also wish to code a passage to identify the structure, such as by placing a code in the margin beside the boxed trigger words, using CH for chronological, C/E for cause and effect, and so on. You might also incorporate key trigger words on anchor charts to further assist students.

### Mini-Lesson 3: Using Graphic Organizers

Conduct mini-lessons on how to use graphic organizers to identify and analyze the structure of a text. Information presented in chronological order can be tracked using a timeline or sequential boxes. Comparisons can easily be charted on a Venn diagram or a Y chart. Cause-and-effect relationships can be shown through simple graphic organizers. In a mini-lesson, you can model and clarify the organizational structure of a passage by pulling out key information from the passage and charting it on a graphic organizer.

**Extending the Skill in the Mini-Lessons:** Keep in mind that many well-written texts include a variety of structures. Preparing students to recognize a mix of structures, describe the purpose of each one, and identify the dominant structure of the overall passage is a better long-term objective for instruction than focusing only on identifying text structure.

**Closing the Mini-Lessons:** The final idea to stress to students is that ideas are conveyed in a structured way. Using strategies to detect and make use of the structure can help students read deeply and enhance their ability to comprehend complex texts.

## Recognizing Point of View

Point of view is another new area of emphasis in most standards. Critical readers must consider who is telling a story or who is presenting the information in a passage. In literature, thinking about who is telling the story, how he or she is telling it, and what information he or she chooses to share helps readers follow the story as it unfolds. Readers must be able to analyze characters and understand their actions and motives. Stories usually unfold through the eyes of a character (first person) or an unnamed narrator (third person). This is a decision authors consider carefully. Attentive readers must examine the storyteller's actions, words, and how other characters react to him or her in order to fully understand what is happening and why. The Point of View Checklist reproducible on page 126 describes features of first-person and third-person narratives, and can be used as a checklist with any of the mini-lessons below. Likewise, all informational texts are filtered through the author's perspective. Critical readers must identify the author's purpose, follow and evaluate his or her line of thinking, and then determine if that purpose has been met.

You'll want to be sure your mini-lessons align with grade-level expectations and address nuances between literature and informational texts. Suggestions for three mini lessons appear below.

## Mini-Lesson 1: Literature: Narrative Performances, Readers Theater Skits, and Multiple Perspective Studies

Reading in the voices of different characters is a good read-aloud activity for early elementary grade students, yet this idea can also be adapted for older students. You can perform a narrative passage as if it were a play by assigning a role to each student (or having students select a role) to read aloud. A narrator reads everything that isn't contained within quotation marks. This process works with all kinds of passages: excerpts from books, such as *Charlotte's Web*, short stories, myths, or realistic fiction.

Select passages with short and lively exchanges of dialogue between characters. Students must recognize when different characters are speaking based on punctuation clues (quotation marks) or a change of speaker. Helping students read expressively, based on prompts in a text or on inferences drawn from a character's words or behavior, is another way to build an awareness of point of view.

**Variations for Literature Mini-Lessons:** Plays and dramas can be an asset among your close reading materials. For example, readers theater has an easy-to-follow structure that helps students recognize which characters are speaking and also cues their dialogue exchanges.

A variation on this activity is to include passages that are told from very different perspectives. For early elementary students, works such as *The True Story of the Three Little Pigs* by Jon Scieszka (1989) and *Seriously, Cinderella is SO Annoying!* by Trisha Speed Shaskan (2011) present novel takes on well-known fairy tales. For our fourth-grade students, we often use a narrative passage told from the point of view of Paul Revere's horse, *"Paul Revere's Ride–On Me"* by Joyce Lansky (AppleSeeds) together with an excerpt from "Paul Revere's Ride" by Henry Wadsworth Longfellow. For upper elementary students, consider using excerpts from *Seedfolks* by Paul Fleischman, which depicts multiple perspectives surrounding the planting of a neighborhood garden.

**Extending the Skill With Literature:** In addition to mastering the basics of who is speaking, who is telling the story, and so on, students should also consider how point of view contributes to the tone or message of the story. Questions to guide reflection and analysis of point of view appear on page 118 together with CCSS grade-level standards.

## Mini-Lesson 2: Informational Text: Scavenger Hunt

Scavenger hunts are a fun way to help students gain skill in analyzing an author's point of view in informational texts. In this type of an activity, students use clues from text features and the text structure to identify the author's purpose. Begin with the title, if it contains clues about the content or the author's take on the subject. Have students underline words or phrases that give clues about the author's purpose and mark them with a lowercase *p*. Next, look for structural clues, which might include trigger words that call out the main points the author makes on the topic. These, too, will help students determine the author's purpose and point of view. In addition, you may want to hunt for words that suggest a value judgment. Anecdotes, stories, or figurative language are other techniques an author might use to express a point. Hunting for quotations, or other types of outside sources that authors sometimes use, is another item you'll want to include on your scavenger hunt. Students should also note the amount of space an author gives to a topic. Important ideas typically are given more space, which is another way to build ideas about the author's purpose. Use these and others that appear in the Take-5 Mini-Lesson on locating and using text evidence that begins on page 115.

**Variations for Informational Text Mini-Lessons:** Excerpts from famous speeches are often good sources for judgment words and varied forms of figurative language. You might also consider drafting a letter or an essay that includes the items you're analyzing. For example, you could write a persuasive letter to the principal, mayor, or president on a topic of interest and highlight where and how you might use the features and techniques you're exploring. Our students have written persuasive letters to our mayor requesting a beautification project for our village. They cited a recent newspaper article about littering as the basis for their request.

**Extending the Skill With Informational Text:** Emphasize that authors of informational text have a viewpoint even if it isn't explicitly stated. Simply by presenting points he or she deems important, an author shapes or filters the information readers take in as they build their knowledge and understanding of a particular topic. In some informational texts, authors want to change readers' thinking in some way or influence their thoughts on topics. Questions to guide reflection and analysis of point of view appear on page 119 with CCSS grade-level standards.

**Closing the Mini-Lessons:** *Literature and Informational Texts:* To sum up, it's important to stress that authors of literature and informational text make careful decisions about point of view. In literature, authors determine who will tell the story, how it will be told, and what information they will share with readers. Authors of informational text express a viewpoint in the content they include in the passage. Their views also determine how they will present information. Recognizing this can help students understand and evaluate complex texts.

## Recognizing Author Intentions

Students may not be aware that all manner of texts result from careful planning. Authors select every word, and every event serves a distinct purpose. Nothing is random. Knowing this, readers must question their own thinking and square their ideas with what they believe the author intended.

Close reading instruction relies on readers reconciling an author's intentions with their own understanding of the text. Doing so helps assure us that we have interpreted a passage in a manner that the author designed and intended for us. Mini-lessons to help support students' understanding and use of this strategy follow.

### *Mini-Lesson 1:* **Meet and Greet the Author**

Begin by discussing the text as if the author were in your classroom: "If Thomas Jefferson were in our classroom, how would he explain his word choice when drafting the Declaration of Independence? What does he mean specifically by using the word *self-evident*? Why is this a critical word choice?" Here's another example: "What would Elizabeth Cady Stanton say if we were to ask her what her intention was to model the Declaration of Rights and Sentiments on the Declaration of Independence?"

## Mini-Lesson 2: "Why Did the Author . . ." Questions and "Swap Out"

A variation on the previous mini-lesson involves questioning an author and determining the suitability of a swap. As an example, in a close reading excerpt from *Charlotte's Web*, such a question might be: *Why did the author begin the story with the following sentence: "'Where's Papa going with that ax?' said Fern to her mother as they were setting the table for breakfast."* The answer to elicit is that the author has crafted a beginning that launches the story's problem. Moreover, it is an irresistible beginning that alarms us and makes us wonder about what's going to happen. We want to learn more and are eager to read on.

After discussing the question and answers, call on a student (or pair or team) to assume the role of the author and ask whether he or she would be willing to swap out a word choice, a character, an event, and so on. In the example above, you might ask the author if he or she would swap the word "ax" for the words "plate of pig food"? The author would then explain his or her answer. Involving the whole class in the discussion helps students think carefully about an author's intention.

**Extending the Mini-Lessons:** Eventually, you will want to integrate a text-marking strategy as students practice and gain skill in recognizing purposeful word choice, strong ideas, and critical events that strike them as strongly author driven. For example, students might place an exclamation mark by the opening sentence of *Charlotte's Web* to capture their immediate reaction to the opening line.

In addition to exploring author intentions for specific elements of a passage, students should reflect on how these intentions help build the overall theme in literature and the main idea/purpose in informational text after they have read and reviewed the entire passage.

**Closing the Mini-Lessons:** *Literature and Informational Texts:* Recount other areas of study that demonstrate an author's purposeful decision-making, such as a choice of text structure and point of view.


# Traditional Strategy Instruction

Well-established reading comprehension strategies provide a practical way to build new standards-based skills. Although many teachers are familiar with these strategies, there are unique ways they can be used to support the rigorous demands of the standards. Covered in this group are the following:

- Finding word meaning and building vocabulary, including academic and domain-specific vocabulary, using context clues
- Comparing and contrasting
- Sequencing
- Identifying theme and main idea

All of these comprehension strategies have been used for many years and remain in good standing among respected literacy experts, including Fountas and Pinnell, Harvey, and others.

Some of these strategies, such as sequencing, are foundational and establish strong reading behaviors in students. They are often considered prerequisites for building other, more complex skills. Typically, students in grades 2–6 either have these strategies in place or are working toward developing them. Other strategies are more sophisticated and may rely on the coordinated use of two or more foundational strategies. For example, identifying the theme or main idea of a passage presumes that students can read and understand it (with some productive struggle), identify important ideas from supporting ideas, and evaluate their understanding. Some quick and easy ways to adapt your use of the strategies appear in the chart on pages 120 and 121. As you'll note, these can be used alongside traditional methods of instruction.

Making use of the multiple readings that goes hand-in-hand with close reading is another tip that is apparent in the chart. Encouraging students to go back and reread a section or the entire passage is extremely beneficial. They have several chances to figure out or clarify meaning, they may see things for the first time and gain new meaning and alter or reshape an idea based on this; and they can build evidence and support for their ideas. Many texts encourage students to reread materials three times and to align their reading expectations with the three main categories of the CCSS: key ideas and details, craft and structure, and integration of knowledge and ideas. Although this is a good recommendation, we've found that returning to a full passage twice and then to particular sections as many times as is needed (to acquire, pull, or extract information for a question or task) is the direction that our instruction has taken.

Although the traditional strategies presented in this section represent just a few of the many that are used, it's important to note that there are others that are equally beneficial to use with your close reading. You might wish to think about ways you could make them align with your current standards. Also, it will be helpful to determine how your students already make use of these traditional strategies. Extending what they already know by helping them apply the strategies to today's standards will help set the direction you should take with your mini-lessons.

After revisiting a traditional strategy and making it square with your standards, the finale involves helping students understand that they can utilize their entire repertoire of strategies to closely read a text.

# *Five Tips* for Teaching These Strategies

1.  **Gauge students' background knowledge, skills, and abilities with these strategies early on.** Having a good idea of how much or how little experience your students have had with any of these strategies is time-saving information that will prevent redundant over-teaching. As you launch and work through the close reading lessons and mini-lessons, size up your students' actions and reactions as well as their ability to use a strategy. Make adjustments to your lessons accordingly: strengthen some (additional mini-lessons or practice) and reduce or eliminate others.

2.  **Most of these strategies spiral in a repetitive cycle in which students learn, practice, gain proficiency, reach mastery, and learn new ways to extend the strategy.** Keeping this cycle in mind, be on the lookout for rich areas to revisit during your authentic close reading instruction. Encourage students to practice a particular strategy so they can build their experience using it authentically.

3.  **Consider ways you can integrate strategy practice with other classroom routines.** To reduce instructional overload, think of ways to integrate or embed close reading strategy practice within other routines your students already follow. For example, if you have a morning drill, alternate new vocabulary, text structure, or text-marking practice with the regular routine. Independent reading time presents the perfect venue for students to authentically practice new strategies. Briefly sharing their experiences with a partner or writing a short entry in a reading journal at the end of a text are further ways they can reflect on the process.

4.  **Positive encouragement and structured support are perfect complements to complex texts.** Setting a tone of success in your classroom can go a long way. As students work with complex passages, they will encounter new challenges. Skilled readers will grapple with the level of deep-reading analysis required of close reading, and struggling readers may, at times, feel overwhelmed. The greater gains that all students can attain are worth the effort. You can help students reach a point where they realize this themselves through your encouragement and support.

5. **Adopt, adapt, and add to these strategies to suit your needs.** The strategies in this chapter can be considered as a good basic collection. Adopt them as they are, adapt them to suit your instructional style and/or your students' needs, and add more strategies as needed.

## Professional Development Activities

Select any one of the Take-5 Mini-Lessons and consider how you might adapt it. Share your ideas with colleagues and start a fruitful dialogue.

Work with a partner or in a small collaborative team using the mini-lesson suggestions provided on pages 99–104 to create a Take-5 Mini-Lesson plan on a strategy to help students build their skills with the following:
- Identifying text structure
- Recognizing point of view
- Recognizing author intentions
- Finding meaning for academic and domain-specific vocabulary
- A strategy of your choice

Share your collection of mini-lessons with colleagues.

Select a traditional reading strategy you feel could be updated to better help students meet the standards. Your update might involve altering the strategy, altering your instruction of the strategy, or both. As a collaborative activity with your colleagues, discuss how you would update your strategy.

# General Guidelines for Building Students' Skill With Text Marking

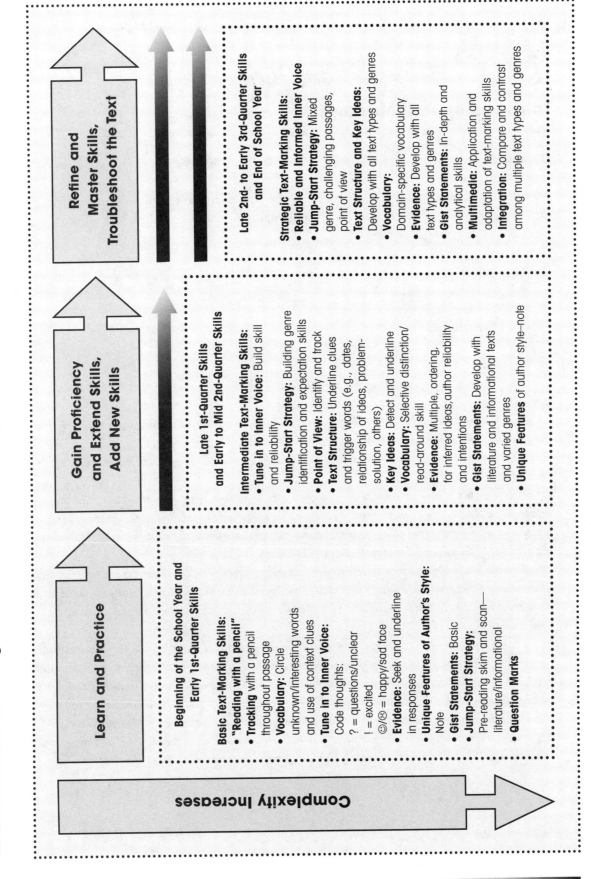

**Learn and Practice**

**Gain Proficiency and Extend Skills, Add New Skills**

**Refine and Master Skills, Troubleshoot the Text**

**Complexity Increases**

## Beginning of the School Year and Early 1st-Quarter Skills

**Basic Text-Marking Skills:**
- **"Reading with a pencil"**
- **Tracking** with a pencil throughout passage
- **Vocabulary:** Circle unknown/interesting words and use of context clues
- **Tune in to Inner Voice:** Code thoughts:
  ? = questions/unclear
  ! = excited
  ☺/☹ = happy/sad face
- **Evidence:** Seek and underline in responses
- **Unique Features of Author's Style:** Note
- **Gist Statements:** Basic
- **Jump-Start Strategy:** Pre-reading skim and scan—literature/informational
- **Question Marks**

## Late 1st-Quarter Skills and Early to Mid 2nd-Quarter Skills

**Intermediate Text-Marking Skills:**
- **Tune in to Inner Voice:** Build skill and reliability
- **Jump-Start Strategy:** Building genre identification and expectation skills
- **Point of View:** Identify and track
- **Text Structure:** Underline clues and trigger words (e.g., dates, relationship of ideas, problem-solution, others)
- **Key Ideas:** Detect and underline
- **Vocabulary:** Selective distinction/read-around skill
- **Evidence:** Multiple, ordering, for inferred ideas, author reliability and intentions
- **Gist Statements:** Develop with literature and informational texts and varied genres
- **Unique Features** of author style–note

## Late 2nd- to Early 3rd-Quarter Skills and End of School Year

**Strategic Text-Marking Skills:**
- **Reliable and Informed Inner Voice**
- **Jump-Start Strategy:** Mixed genre, challenging passages, point of view
- **Text Structure and Key Ideas:** Develop with all text types and genres
- **Vocabulary:** Domain-specific vocabulary
- **Evidence:** Develop with all text types and genres
- **Gist Statements:** In-depth and analytical skills
- **Multimedia:** Application and adaptation of text-marking skills
- **Integration:** Compare and contrast among multiple text types and genres

# *Take-5 Mini-Lesson Plan*
## Introducing Text Marking

**Objective:** To introduce text marking          **Delivery Suggestion:** Early Core Lesson

**Essential Skill Questions:** How can we strengthen our ability to read deeply and analytically during close reading? How can we demonstrate our critical-thinking skills and other interactions we have with a text?

**Guiding Questions:**
- What is text marking?
- Why is it used?
- How is it used?

### Introduction

*Text marking is a way we code our passage while we're reading. You can think of it as "reading with a pencil."*

*Text marking is useful because it helps us track and shape our deep thinking as we're close reading. For example, as we read, we take in and react to information. We also seek and reflect upon information. We piece together a text's meaning using this process: take in, react, seek, and reflect; take in, react, seek, and reflect.*

*Text marking is how we show this process. We may underline, circle, or write letter codes to identify information. Another type of text marking helps us get a clear understanding of the meaning of a sentence or a paragraph. For this type of text marking, we summarize the meaning in our own words in the margins of the passage. This is called a gist statement.*

*Your role is to learn and practice effective text marking. Over time, you'll learn to identify important ideas, words, or other critical findings in a passage and mark them. You'll learn to trust your reactions and mark them accordingly. You'll also connect your thoughts cohesively together in ways that show careful and deep reading.*

*Throughout this lesson, we'll explore two text-marking basics. First, we'll use our pencil to track our reading. This means I should see your pencil moving from left to right across the page as you read. Second, I'd like you to circle unknown or interesting words. These could be words you don't know or words that are interesting to you personally. For example, they may grab your attention, or you may think they are noteworthy or appealing, or they may interest you in others ways that you can describe. Soon, we'll learn how to use clues in a passage to help decipher unknown words. We'll also learn how to build our word banks. For now, though, we're just going to identify words by circling them.*

**Start-Up Activity:** Prepare a Text-Marking Skills Chart patterned after the first three bulleted items in the "Beginning of the School Year and Early 1st-Quarter Skills" box on page 107. Begin with these items and add others as you introduce them through mini-lessons. You may also want to have students quickly draw a box containing the key for the text codes. This is helpful as students build skill with text marking, yet is a temporary aid that should be eliminated as they gain proficiency and automaticity.

*Let's get started by drawing a quick one inch-by-one inch box on the cover of your passage. In it, we'll write "Track with a pencil" and below that we'll draw a circle followed by the word "vocabulary," which means we'll circle interesting or unusual vocabulary words.* (After a few minutes, direct students to the planned close reading lesson where they will begin their text marking activities.)

**Follow-Through Tips:** As students begin their independent reading, move around the classroom and scan their tracking and text marking. Note areas in need of fixing up (such as those below and on the next page). You might opt to use the break-in or pause moments below during the read-aloud time of your lesson. Then you can model your expectations and briefly discuss fix-ups.

| Break-in or Pause Moments | Dialogue Prompts |
| --- | --- |
| Over/Under Text Marking or Text Marking Used as a Distracter | *I want to pause the lesson and share how I text marked my passage. I observed all of you tracking your reading with your pencil. Great! But, knowing how much or how little text to mark is tricky. Some passages might have a lot of rich words and others might have only a few. For this passage, I found the following X words (specify unknown from interesting). Some of yours might be the same and some might be different. That's okay. I expect that there will be differences. As long as your marking helps you—that's what's important. It's a tool to keep you engaged and focused, and it helps you construct meaning. Over or under text marking can take away its usefulness. Also, you don't want your text marking to interfere with your reading and become a distraction. Soon, we'll learn how to use clues in a passage to help decipher unknown words. We'll also learn how to build our word banks. For now, take 15 seconds each and share your selection with an elbow partner. Reflect on your own choices and gauge whether you've marked too much, too little, or just the right amount of text. Give me a thumbs-up if you can self-assess your work and know how you might adjust your marking, if you wanted to.* |

| Break-in or Pause Moments | Dialogue Prompts |
| --- | --- |
| Writing a Gist Statement | *Now, I'd like to model how to write a gist statement. Remember, a gist statement is a summary of some portion of the text that we write using mostly our own words. This helps us clarify our understanding. I'm going to compose a brief gist statement for the first paragraph.* (Model statement.) *Think about the features that make this a good gist statement and be prepared to share your ideas.* (Example: Gist statements are brief, capture key ideas, mostly written in own words, summarize ideas.) *Give me a thumbs-up if you've assessed the features that make this a good gist statement and could write your own for a paragraph from tomorrow's reading. Now we've practiced a few very basic text-marking skills—there are many others we'll learn over time—so let's return to our lesson.* |

**Extending the Skill:** Text marking is a general strategy that supports many other strategies. You'll extend its use as students learn other strategies and as they adapt their text marking to a variety of genres and text types. The diagram on page 107 presents a good progression of strategies to follow. Other Take-5 Mini-Lessons appearing in this chapter are useful for text marking and are noted as such. Suggestions for other mini-lessons that appear in this chapter may also piggyback off this lesson. They, too, can be adapted to fit this Take-5 Mini-Lesson format.

**Closing the Planned Lesson:** *Now that we've completed today's close reading lesson, let's return to our Take-5 Mini-Lesson and review what text marking is and how we used it to build our close reading skills.*

**Key Indicators of Success/Need for Individual or Small-Group Instruction:** Students demonstrate ease with tracking and text marking a reasonable number of appropriate words. Should students need more guidance, determine if a brief one-on-one conference is called for or provide scaffolded assistance during small-group instruction.

# Take-5 Mini-Lesson Plan
## Introducing the Jump-Start Strategy

**Objective:** To introduce the jump-start strategy    **Delivery Suggestion:** Early Core Lesson

**Essential Skill Question:** How can the jump-start pre-reading strategy help me launch my close reading skills?

**Guiding Question:**
- What is the jump-start strategy?
- Why is it used?
- How is it used?

### Introduction

*The jump-start strategy is a pre-reading strategy that gets us revved up and ready to read. It's useful because it gives us a lot of helpful information about the passage before we begin reading. It sparks our ideas, such as what the passage might be about, its genre, how it's organized, and more. It also helps us set logical expectations, which we'll check as we read.*

*You activate the jump-start strategy right before you begin reading by quickly skimming and scanning a passage. All the while, you're detecting and collecting clues to help spark your ideas and set your expectations about your reading. Your role is also to apply what you've learned previously and to practice applying new knowledge we're learning in class.*

*Throughout this lesson, we'll explore the basics of our jump-start strategy. We're going to try and detect the genre—literature or informational text. Based on this and on our grade-level knowledge of the genre, we're also going to set some expectations.*

**Start-Up Activity:** Use a section of the Jump-Start Checklist (page 125) to introduce students to the features they can use to help distinguish literature from informational texts.

*Let's get started by identifying things we might look for in a passage that could suggest the genre— literature or informational text. I have a checklist of many of these features. Let's see if we can name them all.*

*Before you begin your independent reading, would you take about 10 seconds and skim and scan the passage for the items on our checklist? Take in as much as you can: What do you see on the page? Can you spot some text that's short and easy to read? Give me a thumbs-up if you think you can identify the genre. Then text mark alongside the title an "L" for literature or an "I" for informational text. We will learn over time how to set expectations based on what we know about the genre of a passage. We'll also share ideas in our discussions. (After a few minutes, direct students to the planned close reading lesson.)*

**Follow-Through Tips:** After you read through the text (and prior to beginning the questions and tasks), discuss the clues students used to generate their ideas about the genre. As you move to the questions and tasks during your planned close reading lesson, integrate further discussion about genre. You may want to break in to or pause the lesson to explain and model some of your expectations or to assist students as needed. The chart below shows some common break-in moments you might cover.

| Break-in or Pause Moments | Dialogue Prompts |
|---|---|
| Identification of Features | *Did you notice the illustrations on the cover that might have suggested this was a work of literature—perhaps a short story? I also did a quick read of the title and suspect it is a story. Did you spy other things?* |
| Setting Expectations | *I want to briefly share how we might use our knowledge of genre to set expectations. In this passage, which I suspect is a work of literature, I will be prepared to look for characters, a problem or conflict, and events that lead to a solution. I expect these elements because I know that most stories contain them.* |

**Extending the Skill:** Depending on students' background knowledge, you can extend the features that they notice (from the chart you compose using the Jump-Start Checklist). You might also incorporate expectations based on text structure, such as in the second example above.

**Closing the Planned Lesson:** *Now that we've completed today's close reading lesson, let's return to our Take-5 Mini-Lesson and share a couple of thoughts about our jump-start strategy and how we can make good use of it as we gain knowledge and experience with genres. Who would like to share their thoughts?*

**Key Indicators of Success/Need for Small-Group Instruction:** Students should demonstrate a beginning level of skill with the jump-start strategy. Identifying some features that can help them select a genre is key. Also, they should be able to express an understanding of the value of using the jump-start process. This will be apparent during your class discussions. If students are unable to identify the genre after your Day 1 reading, you may need to provide scaffolded assistance during small-group instruction.

# Take-5 Mini-Lesson Plan

## Listening to My Inner Voice

**Objective:** To introduce the inner-voice strategy     **Delivery Suggestion:** Early Core Lesson

**Essential Skill Question:** How can listening to my inner voice help me launch and monitor my close reading skills and reading comprehension?

**Guiding Questions:**
- What is my inner voice?
- Why is it used?
- How is it used?

### Introduction

*Listening to your inner voice is like having a conversation with yourself about your ideas, only the conversation is kept in your head.*

*It's useful because the conversation or dialogue you have about your close reading keeps your ideas in check and helps guide your thinking. It also helps you direct your use of other close reading strategies you learn.*

*The way it's used is simple. As you take in information from your reading—ideas, events, characters, critical ideas, and so on—your inner voice is helping you piece it together, organize it, and clarify it. You might ask yourself questions, or react expressively, like saying "Wow!" in your head. Other times, you might take direction from your inner voice, such as by saying "Gosh, I wonder what strategy I can use to help me keep all of this information straight? I know, I'll use my text-marking skills!" There are many ways to use your inner voice.*

*Your role is to start listening to your inner voice during your close reading. Then, begin to dialogue back and forth with your inner voice. Keep it focused and attentive on what you're reading. Soon, your inner voice will become automatic—and will kick in as you need it to help you build meaning.*

*Throughout this lesson, we'll explore ways to listen to our inner voice. I would like you to listen to your inner voice as you read silently. Focus your inner voice and spark some dialogue by launching your jump-start clues. Think about ways you can guide your thinking as you speculate about the genre and more.*

**Start-Up Activity:** Share the Probing a Passage chart (page 96) with students. Begin with the jump-start and move to the monitoring section as students learn more strategies.

*Let's get started by quickly reviewing some prompts you might ask yourself as you work through the jump-start strategy. Remember to text mark a code "L" for literature and "I" for informational text alongside the title.* (After a few minutes, direct students to the planned close reading lesson.)

*Close Reading for the Whole Class* • © 2015 by Sandra K. Athans & Denise Ashe Devine • Scholastic Teaching Resources     **113**

**Follow-Through Tips:** Prior to beginning your reading, you might want to have students break into pairs or teams and briefly share their experiences. Monitoring their ideas will help guide your modeling of the strategy as you perform your teacher reading of the passage. Use the break-in or pause moments in the chart below to further model ways you use your inner voice and dialogue to help make meaning.

| Break-in or Pause Moments | Dialogue Prompts |
| --- | --- |
| Example | *I'm going to pause from my reading to demonstrate the kind of inner dialogue I have as I close read my passage. "Gosh, I think the genre I suspected is correct. Based on my reading, I can confirm that the passage is informational text."* (Model another example.) *Now, I'd like to model another example . . .* |

**Extending the Skill:** As students learn new strategies, model the kind of dialogue that could take place as you use each strategy. This is especially true with some of the new areas of emphasis in the CCSS and other standards.

**Closing the Planned Lesson:** *Now that we've completed today's close reading lesson, let's return to our Take-5 Mini-Lesson and share a couple of thoughts about how we used our inner voice to help us make and monitor meaning.*

**Key Indicators of Success/Need for Small-Group Instruction:** Students should demonstrate a beginning level of skill with the inner-voice strategy. One way to monitor students' success is to review their text marking, which will demonstrate how they've used their inner voice. Another way to check is to conference with students during small-group instruction and/or to ask them to demonstrate the skill aloud. If students struggle with this, continue teacher and peer modeling and provide opportunities for continued practice.

# *Take-5 Mini-Lesson Plan*

## Locating and Using Evidence

**Objective:** To strengthen skill with evidence.　　**Delivery Suggestion:** Early-Mid Core Lesson

**Essential Skill Question:** What tips and techniques can help me locate and use evidence effectively?

**Guiding Questions:**

- What can be used as evidence?
- How can I use evidence?
- How can I tell which evidence is best to use?
- How do I use this strategy?

**Note:** You may want to refer to earlier passages or other reading material (this lesson works well with a mixed-genre passage, such as an informational article about folktales that also includes a folktale or paired passages, such as a poem and a biography about the poet).

### Introduction

*We already know a lot about evidence because we've used it in all of our close reading lessons. Today, we're going to summarize key ideas we've already learned about evidence and also learn new tips and techniques for getting even better at finding and using it. Strengthening these skills will help us strengthen our ideas.*

*Evidence can be found in many places in a passage: the text and illustrations, photographs, captions, data tables, footnotes, and other text features. As a general rule of thumb, it's best to have two to three pieces of evidence to support your ideas, whenever possible. It's also important to think about which evidence is the best, or in other words, the most convincing. The strongest evidence you have should be used first when you're answering questions either in writing or in discussions.*

*Your role now is to scour today's passage to locate all the evidence for our discussion questions, and then to judge which is the strongest, next strongest, and so on. This is called ranking the evidence. You'll share your thinking aloud and explain how you ranked each piece of evidence.*

**Start-Up Activity:** You may want to use a head-start anchor chart (such as the one below) or scribe broad categories of evidence on chart paper. This can become an anchor chart that can be updated as you encounter unique new sources of evidence.

---

### Tips and Techniques for Finding Evidence

1. There are many sources of evidence:
   *Text • Illustrations • Quotations • Data in Tables, Charts, and Diagrams • Footnotes • Author's Note • Captions*
2. Not all evidence is equal: Use good, fact-based judgment or reasoning to weigh evidence.
3. Weigh evidence based on facts—not on your opinion or likes and dislikes: Detect and reject personal opinion!
4. Seek likely and reasonable evidence for your inferences.

*Let's get started by going on an Evidence Scavenger Hunt. To do this, identify all the text features and elements you see in today's passage that could be a source of evidence. Keep a list in your head. In a minute we'll briefly share our ideas and add them to our chart. After that, we'll read the passage as usual. Then, as you answer the questions, you'll locate all of the evidence that supports your ideas. Next, you'll rank the evidence.* (After a minute, record students' ideas and ensure that all elements in the passage have been identified.)

**Follow-Through Tips:** After you read through the passage (and prior to beginning the questions and tasks), emphasize the multiple sources that could be used as evidence. As you begin the discussion to answer the text-based questions, follow a routine protocol of encouraging students to do the following:

- Identify all evidence
- Rank the evidence and share their reasoning

Break in to or pause the lessons to explain and model some of your expectations or to assist students as needed. The chart below contains common break-in moments you might cover.

| Break-in or Pause Moments | Dialogue Prompts |
|---|---|
| Use all elements of the passage as sources for evidence | *Although some sources of evidence are pretty clear, others may not be. For instance, could you use the way a character responds to another as evidence? As an example, could the fact that Bill didn't want to sit near Riley during lunch help support an idea we have about Bill or Riley? Could you use an author's word choice as a form of evidence? For example, Riley's "untidy" eating habits are quite different from his "ghastly" eating habits.* (Help students identify hidden pieces of evidence.) |
| Weigh evidence | *Determining why one piece of evidence may be more compelling than another may take practice. Sometimes it's easy to figure out which evidence is the strongest. The author might tell us directly with key words like "most important," or the author might have already listed and ranked the evidence. Other times, however, it can be tricky to weigh evidence. Looking at how much emphasis an author places on the evidence is one way to figure this out. Other points the author makes elsewhere in text might also help you rank evidence.* |
| Weigh evidence based on facts and the author's intentions (keeping connections and personal opinion in check) | *Sometimes the way we connect to a passage might get in the way of how we judge evidence. For example, if an author writes an article about popular pets, we might unintentionally think that the type of pet each of us owns is the one the author suggests is most popular. We can easily get sidetracked by our opinions, likes and dislikes, and personal experiences. It's important to stick to the facts and recognize these distracters.* |

| Break-in or Pause Moments | Dialogue Prompts |
| --- | --- |
| Build evidence for inferences | *When the author doesn't tell us something directly and we instead must use inferencing (or reading between the lines), we must still build a case for our views. Determining likely reasons for our thinking is necessary. Ask yourself: "Based on a detail, fact, event, or idea expressed in the text, is my idea likely and/or reasonable?"* |

**Extending the Skills:** As students explore a variety of passages, they may encounter other ways to apply these skills. Adding on to an anchor chart will help them grasp the flexible, yet powerful, ways evidence can be used to support their views. Also, students must develop skills to determine if the author presents credible evidence. Providing direct instruction on this is an excellent extension of these skills.

**Closing the Planned Lesson:** *Now that we've completed today's close reading lesson, let's return to our Take-5 Mini-Lesson and share a couple of thoughts about our ability to locate and use evidence. From today's discussions, it's clear that we're strengthening our skills with evidence. If I were to summarize your successes into a "Can-Do" checklist, it would contain the following:*

- *I can support my ideas with strong evidence.*
- *I can identify my strongest evidence and present it well.*
- *I can use multiple pieces of evidence, especially to support my inferences.*

**Key Indicators of Success/Need for Small-Group Instruction:** Students should demonstrate proficiency with fundamental skills of finding and using evidence from earlier lessons. Here, they should be able to identify some of the less common forms of evidence, express the reasoning behind their ranking, monitor their ability to detect and reject personal opinions and other distracters, and build likely and reasonable evidence for their inferences.

# Questions to Guide Student Reflection and Discussion on the Use and Effects of Point of View in Literature

| CCSS Standard 6: *Assess how point of view or purpose shapes the content and style of a text.* | Grade 2 | Grade 3 | Grade 4 | Grade 5 | Grade 6 |
|---|---|---|---|---|---|
| Literature | Acknowledge differences in the points of view of characters, including by speaking in a different voice for each character when reading dialogue aloud.<br><br>*Questions:*<br>How would X sound?<br><br>How would Y sound?<br><br>How does X show emotion in his voice? (punctuation, word choice, capitalized or italicized letters, hesitation stuttering, expression, interjections)<br><br>How does Y show emotion in his voice? | Distinguish their own point of view from that of the narrator or those of the characters.<br><br>*Questions:*<br>Do you share the same view as X?<br><br>Do you think differently than Y?<br><br>Would you agree or disagree with X?<br><br>In your opinion, is X right or wrong in thinking that?<br><br>Do you see things like X?<br><br>Would you have done the same as Y? | Compare and contrast the point of view from which different stories are narrated, including the difference between first- and third-person narrations.<br><br>*Questions:*<br>Who is telling the story? (What pronouns are used by the narrator?)<br><br>What insights are you given into a character's thoughts and feelings? | Describe how a narrator or speaker's point of view influences how events are described.<br><br>*Questions:*<br>What causes X to say that?<br><br>Why does Y think that?<br><br>Why does X act that way?<br><br>What influences Y? | Explain how an author develops the point of view of the narrator or speaker in a text.<br><br>*Questions:*<br>What events contribute to X's views?<br><br>What events lead to Y's action? |

# Questions to Guide Student Reflection and Discussion on the Use and Effects of Point of View in Informational Text

| CCSS Standard 6: *Assess how point of view or purpose shapes the content and style of a text.* | Grade 2 | Grade 3 | Grade 4 | Grade 5 | Grade 6 |
|---|---|---|---|---|---|
| **Informational Text** | Identify the main purpose of a text, including what the author wants to answer, explain, or describe.<br><br>*Questions:*<br>Why did the author write this?<br><br>Did the author write this to:<br>• Inform the reader?<br>• Explain something?<br>• Convey information?<br><br>What can you gain from reading and analyzing this passage?<br><br>In this informational text, what point does the author make?<br><br>Can you tell the author's feelings about the subject (even if he or she hasn't stated them in the passage)? | Distinguish their own point of view from that of the author of a text.<br><br>*Questions:*<br>Do you share the same view as the author?<br><br>Do you think differently than the author?<br><br>Would you agree/disagree with the author? In your opinion, is the author right or wrong in thinking that…?<br><br>Do you see things like the author?<br><br>Would you have included the same information as the author? | Compare and contrast a firsthand and secondhand account of the same event or topic; describe the differences in the focus and the information provided.<br><br>*Questions:*<br>Who is providing the information? (What pronouns are used by the author?)<br><br>Was the author present at the time of the event?<br><br>Is the information based on what the author observed?<br><br>Is the author reporting an event that he/she did not attend or observe?<br><br>How do the accounts of the events compare?<br><br>What is the same and what is different about the accounts? | Analyze multiple accounts of the same event or topic, noting important similarities and differences in the point of view they represent.<br><br>*Questions:*<br>Who is providing the information?<br><br>What is his/her account?<br><br>How does his/her account compare to other accounts?<br><br>On what does he/she base his or her account? | Determine an author's point of view or purpose in a text and explain how it is conveyed in the text.<br><br>*Questions:*<br>What is the author's point of view?<br><br>Is the author's view reflected in:<br>• Word choice?<br>• Quantity of coverage?<br>• Content included?<br>• Content excluded?<br>• Type of resources?<br>• Order of content?<br>• Order of resources? |

## CCSS Adaptations for Traditional Strategy Instruction

| Strategy | Description/Traditional Methods of Instruction | CCSS Adaptations and Updates |
|---|---|---|
| **Finding word meaning and building vocabulary using context clues** | Students are continually coming across new and unknown words. Helping them develop strategies for building word recognition and vocabulary remains a focused initiative.<br><br>*Techniques:* Sounding out, chunking, and linking words to others are methods that help support the use of context clues to make meaning of words or phrases. | Standard 4 calls for students to interpret words and phrases used in a text. *Circling unknown words and "reading around" them to make meaning is helpful. Assist students in building flexible and ongoing understanding. Returning to the text several times and rereading is beneficial.*<br><br>A major shift in the standards addresses the use of academic vocabulary. This includes pivotal and commonly found words instead of obscure terms. *Focusing on relevant words while revisiting your existing vocabulary lists and instruction is a start. New avenues presented in the Language standards emphasize direct instruction in word patterns and structure, Greek and Latin roots, and other word study skills.*<br><br>Students in Grade 6 and above read and learn from content-area texts, which influence their work with word recognition and vocabulary development. *Authentic, repeated exposure to and manipulation of these words in the content areas is beneficial.* |
| **Comparing and contrasting** | Considering ways in which ideas relate to something else—either through similarities or differences—helps develop understanding.<br><br>*Techniques:* Venn diagrams and other graphic organizers | Students are comparing and contrasting new areas such as point of view, primary and secondary sources, and more. *Use traditional graphic organizers to explore new areas. Also, help students phrase and transition their comparisons. Consider ways to use simple T-charts, charts, and other graphic organizers for comparisons of multiple texts. Returning to the text several times and rereading is beneficial.* |
| **Sequencing** | Making sense of the order in which ideas are presented enables students to build comprehension.<br><br>*Techniques:* Signal words | As students read more complex and/or dense texts (e.g., historical), they may benefit from new techniques. Also, students are using sequence in new ways such as when analyzing text structure, which helps them set expectations for reading (jump-start strategy). They may also use it to determine an author's point of view and purpose for presenting information in a certain way. *Using text-marking boxes and other strategies to call out sequenced text is helpful for guiding and self-monitoring. Practice with a variety of text types is also helpful. Returning to the text several times and rereading is beneficial.* |

## CCSS Adaptations for Traditional Strategy Instruction *continued*

| Strategy | Description/Traditional Methods of Instruction | CCSS Adaptations and Updates |
|---|---|---|
| **Identifying the theme and main idea** | The important idea is the point or message conveyed in the passage. It is what the passage is mostly about.<br><br>*Techniques:* Helping students to recognize the important overall idea is often done by bringing together the elements (such as through a story map) and cohesively looking at the big picture and larger lesson.<br><br>Another approach is to construct the main idea after determining key details or facts (T-chart of key facts) and then blending them together into a cohesive understanding. | Standard 2 specifically asks students to locate and describe a central message or theme within literature and the main topic or main idea of informational text. Keeping the terms aligned to their respective text types is helpful for students.<br><br>Also, students must support their ideas with evidence that must square with an author's intentions. This could suggest a more stringent approach to an already complex task. *Developing students' skills with ordering evidence and distinguishing point of view is helpful.*<br><br>Identifying the essence of a passage is more difficult with complex texts. Encouraging students to look over their text-marked passages should help them reflect on the many strategies they've used while close reading the text. *Using everything they've got will help guide them to the correct identification of theme or main idea.* |

Source: *Quality Comprehension: A Strategic Model of Reading Instruction Using Read–Along Guides, Grades 3–6* (Athans & Devine, 2008).

# --- Close Reading Text Checklist ---

Title _____ Author _____

Source _____ Length _____

1. **Literature or Informational** (circle one); **Genre:** _____

Comments: _____

_____

2. **Text Complexity Measures:**

A. **Quantitative  Lexile Level:** _____

(word/sentence length, syllable count)

| | Below Range | Within Range | Above Range |
|---|---|---|---|
| | ( ) | ( ) | ( ) |

Comments: _____

_____

_____

B. **Qualitative Measures**

(e.g., student exposure, text structure, language conventions, knowledge demands, and so on)

| | Low Complexity | Moderate Complexity | High Complexity |
|---|---|---|---|
| | ( ) | ( ) | ( ) |

Comments: _____

_____

_____

C. **Reader and Task Considerations**

(e.g., motivation, engagement, attitude)

| | Low Appeal | Moderate Appeal | High Appeal |
|---|---|---|---|
| | ( ) | ( ) | ( ) |

Comments: _____

_____

_____

3. **Standards Alignment and 5S Teacher Read Analysis**

A. Key Ideas and Details _____

_____

B. Craft and Structure _____

_____

C. Integration of Knowledge _____

_____

# --- Instructional Unit Plan ---

Thematic Unit: _____  Length of Time: _____

Essential Question: _____

Skills and Strategies: _____

**Close Read Passages** (about 3 days each):

1. _____

Notes:_____

_____

Genre and Structure: _____

**2.** _____

Notes:_____

_____

Genre and Structure: _____

**3.** _____

Notes:_____

_____

Genre and Structure: _____

**Small-Group Instruction:** (skills practice, mini-lessons, close reading support):

| Group 1 | Group 2 | Group 3 |
|---------|---------|---------|
|         |         |         |

**Culminating Activity:** _____

_____

**Standards:** _____

# --- Close Read Guide Rubric ---

Name_____Date_____

Title/Author:_____

**Independent Reading:** Student exhibits engagement with the text:

- Demonstrates sustained focus and attention      **1   2   3   4**
- Employs text marking and rereading      **1   2   3   4**
- Pays careful attention to all text and support features.      **1   2   3   4**

Comments: _____

_____

**Collaborative Discussion:** Student exhibits engagement in the discussion:

- Contributes evidence-based ideas      **1   2   3   4**
  clearly and concisely
- Demonstrates effective listening skills      **1   2   3   4**
- Considers classmates' views      **1   2   3   4**
  and opinions

Comments: _____

_____

**Tasks/Written Responses:** Student exhibits engagement with tasks/written responses:

- Completes assigned tasks/responses      **1   2   3   4**
- Addresses all parts of a task/response      **1   2   3   4**
- Demonstrates consistent effort      **1   2   3   4**
- Applies grade-level language standards      **1   2   3   4**
  in written responses

Comments: _____

_____

**Progressing Toward Independence**      **1   2   3   4**
**With Close Reading Skills:**

> **4** = Consistently exceeds expected performance
> **3** = Demonstrates successful performance
> **2** = Progressing toward successful performance with difficulty
> **1** = Not showing progress toward successful performance

# --- Jump-Start Clues Checklist ---

| Jump-Start Activity | Common Features and Formats: Literature | Common Features and Formats: Informational Text |
|---|---|---|
| **1. Take a Visual Inventory** <br> Scan a passage and take in as much as you can. <br> (For a multiple-page passage, quickly scan the first two or three pages.) <br> **Notice:** Telling features and layout formats, such as artwork, figures, number of columns, unusual spacing, and so on | ____ Illustrations, comics, imaginary visuals <br> ____ Absence of subheadings <br> ____ Single- or two-column prose format; text flows left to right <br> ____ Poetry: lines and stanzas format <br> ____ Drama: listing of cast and dialogue format | ____ Photographs, maps, charts, graphs, diagrams, sidebars (multiple pieces of information on a page) <br> ____ Subheadings <br> ____ One-to-three-column format <br> ____ Interview in question-and-answer format |
| **2. Go on a Quest for Quick Reads** <br> Skim the page, quickly reading *exhibited** text including the *title (and subtitle)*. <br> ***Notice:** Enlarged, bold, attention-seeking, called out, or ornamental snippets of text | ____ Title/subtitle suggests a work of literature. <br> ____ Callouts (e.g., character dialogue, narration) <br> ____ **Cue words:** *imaginary, fiction, make-believe, fantasy, myth, folktale, legend, fable, drama, play, adventures of, beliefs* <br> ____ **Other cues:** Fictitious names, places, and events or occurrences | ____ Title/subtitle suggests informational text. <br> ____ Quick Read subheadings, captions, callouts (e.g., quotations, facts, statistics) <br> ____ Other exhibited text: Note to Reader, boldface vocabulary words, footnotes <br> ____ **Cue words:** *biography, autobiography, history, science, study, research, an account, experience, life of, speech, memoir, argument, true, nonfiction, real life, official, exploring, learning, recognizing,* and so on <br> ____ **Other cues:** well-known personality or famous person, real place, actual event |
| **3. Determine a Genre** <br> Based on Activities 1 and 2, suggest a likely genre: literature or informational. (Where do most of your checks fall?) | ____ Visual inventory and Quick Reads suggest a work of literature. | ____ Visual inventory and Quick Reads suggest a nonfiction or an informational text. |
| **4. Narrow the Genre Further** <br> Using your grade-level know-how, can you make a distinction between the text types? | ____ Stories <br> ____ Poetry <br> ____ Drama <br> ____ Other: _____ | ____ Biography/Autobiography <br> ____ Speech <br> ____ Historical informational <br> ____ Scientific/Technical informational <br> ____ Essays on art or literature <br> ____ Other: _____ |
| **5. Scope out Expectations** <br> Use your knowledge of genre, text structure, and your experiences and background knowledge to set expectations. | ____ I know what this genre is about. (I'll use my genre knowledge.) <br> ____ I know how this genre will be organized. (I'll use my text structure knowledge.) <br> ____ I know what I might expect to find in this genre. (I'll look for special features.) <br> ____ I know how to read this genre. (I'll use special reading tips.) <br> ____ I'll think of what else I know that could help me. (I'll call upon my experiences and background knowledge.) | ____ I know what this genre is about. (I'll use my genre knowledge.) <br> ____ I know how this genre will be organized. (I'll use my text structure knowledge.) <br> ____ I know what I might expect to find in this genre. (I'll look for special features.) <br> ____ I know how to read this genre. (I'll use special reading tips.) <br> ____ I'll think of what else I know that could help me. (I'll call upon my experiences and background knowledge.) |

Name_____Date_____

# --- Point of View Checklist ---

| | First-Person Point of View | Third-Person Point of View |
|---|---|---|
| **Description** | ___ The story is told by the main character.<br>___ The story unfolds as the character tells it to a reader. | ___ The story is told by a narrator who is not a character in the story.<br>___ The story is *reported*. |
| **Clues** | ___ Uses the pronouns *I, me, mine, we*<br>___ Readers know the narrator's thoughts and feelings well because the narrator shares them.<br>___ Clues: *I thought…, I knew…, I felt…, I was angry, sad, happy,* and so on<br>___ Events in the story are told only through that character's perspective—what that character sees, observes, and perceives.<br>  • *I saw…*<br>  • *I noticed…*<br>  • *I watched…*<br>  • *I guessed that…*<br>  • *I'd describe it as…* | ___ Uses the pronouns *he, she, they* or a named character<br>___ Readers may feel a little distanced from the character(s) even when the narrator informs readers of the character(s) thoughts and feelings.<br>___ Clues: *The character(s) thought, the character(s) felt, the character(s) looked angry, sad, happy,* and so on.<br>___ Events in the story may be told through multiple characters giving readers a broader understanding of events:<br>  • *Bear saw the moon and thought…*<br>  • *Fish saw the moon and thought…*<br>  • *Bird saw the moon and thought…* |
| **Example** | *I dug into my backpack and pushed my notebooks, gloves, and scarf to one side. I was starving and couldn't wait for lunchtime. Suddenly I spied a slightly smashed box of raisins underneath my pencil box. I'm not crazy about raisins, but I gobbled them up as if I hadn't eaten in weeks.* | *Jared rummaged in his backpack. Snack time was nearly over, and Cynthia and Dale, who were seated next to him, had just finished their snacks. They were eager to get back to their spelling activity. All at once, Jared smiled, as he pulled a box of raisins from his backpack. He opened the box flap, tilted back his head, and poured the raisins into his mouth.* |
| **Reader Responsibilities** | Even though the narrator seems chummy, the readers must still size him or her up.<br><br>Based on what the character tells me, shows me, and perceives …<br>  • Is he or she trustworthy?<br>  • Are his or her views reliable?<br>  • Are his or her words supported by actions?<br>  • Are his or her motives clear?<br><br>Are there other clues that help me size up the narrator and the story?<br>  • How do other characters respond to him or her?<br>  • What might I know that can help me grasp details in the story? | Readers may be distanced from the characters and events and have to piece together meaning through clues or inferences.<br>  • What do I know about the character(s) based on his/her/their actions or words?<br>  • Does the narrator give me other clues to explain a character's motives or events in the story?<br>  • Are there other clues that help me or other knowledge I have that can help me make sense of the story? |

# References

Athans, S. (2013). *Tales from the top of the world: Climbing Mount Everest with Pete Athans.* Minneapolis, MN: Millbrook Press.

Athans, S. K., & Devine, D. A. (2008). *Quality comprehension: A strategic model of reading instruction using read-along guides, Grades 3–6.* Newark, DE: International Reading Association.

Baum, L. F. (1900). *The wonderful wizard of Oz.* Chicago: George M. Hill Co.

Berleth, R. J. (1990). *Samuel's choice.* New York: Scholastic.

Crout, G. C. (1982). *Miami Valley vignettes.* Middletown, OH: Middletown Historical Society.

DiCamillo, K. (2000). *Because of Winn-Dixie.* Somerville, MA: Candlewick Press.

Fleischman, P. (1997). *Seedfolks.* New York: HarperCollins.

Howe, H. (2012). *Historical collections of Ohio.* London: Forgotten Books.

Kellogg, S. (1984). *Paul Bunyan.* New York: HarperCollins.

Kellogg, S. (1998). *Mike Fink.* Logan, IA: Perfection Learning.

Lansky, J. (2011, May/June). Paul Revere's ride—on me. *AppleSeeds, 13*, pp. 22–23.

Lin, G. (2009). *Where the mountain meets the moon.* New York: Little, Brown.

Longfellow, H. W. [n.d] Paul Revere's ride. Academy of American Poets. Retrieved from http://poets.org/poetsorg/poem/paul-reveres-ride.

Markle, S. (2008). *Animal heroes: True rescue stories.* Minneapolis, MN: Millbrook Press.

McCall, G., & Regan, L. (2011). *Dragons and serpents.* New York: Gareth Stevens.

National Assessment Governing Board. (2008). *Reading framework for the 2009 National Assessment of Educational Progress.* Washington, DC: U.S. Government Printing Office.

National Governors Association Center for Best Practices & Council of Chief State School Officers. (2010). Common Core State Standards for English Language Arts and Literacy and History/Social Studies, Science, and Technical Subjects. Washington, DC: National Governors Association Center for Best Practices, Council of Chief State School Officers.

O'Hern, K, & Walsh, F. (2006). *The Montgomery bus boycott.* New York: Gareth Stevens.

Pimentel, S. (2012). The Common Core State Standards: Priorities for Action [PowerPoint slides]. The Common Core State Standards: Secondary Protocol 3b: Text Complexity—Literacy Across the Content Areas, p. 28.

Rajczak, K. (2011). *Rescue dogs.* New York: Gareth Stevens.

Randolph, J. (2003). *The Iroquois League.* New York: Rosen Publishing Group.

Reber, J. (1998). *The Eerie Canal.* Unionville, NY: Trillium Press.

Robb, L. (February 12, 2014). Teach kids to build their own prior knowledge. MiddleWeb. Retrieved from http://www.middleweb.com/13223/teach-students-build-prior-knowledge.

Scieszka, J. (1989). *The true story of the three little pigs.* New York: Viking Penguin.

Shaskan, T. S. (2011). *Seriously, Cinderella is SO annoying: The story of Cinderella as told by the wicked stepmother.* North Mankato, MN: Picture Window Books.

Soto-Hinman, I., & Hetzel, J. (2009). *The literacy gaps: Bridge-building strategies for English language learners.* Thousand Oaks, CA: Corwin.

Steinbeck, J. (1939). *The grapes of wrath.* New York: The Viking Press.

Stewart, T. (2012, February). The champion of quiet. *Highlights, 67*(24), pp. 26–27.

Sweet, M. (2011). *Balloons over Broadway.* New York: Houghton Mifflin Harcourt.

Taylor, M. D. (1976). *Roll of thunder, hear my cry.* New York: Penguin Putnam.

White, E. B. (1952). *Charlotte's web.* New York: HarperCollins.

Winter, J. (2009). *Nasreen's secret school: A true story from Afghanistan.* New York: Simon & Schuster.

# Literacy Resources

New York State Education Department: http://www.engageny.org

Massachusetts Department of Education: http://doe.mass.edu

Georgia Department of Education: www.gadoe.org

Partnership for Assessment of Readiness for College and Careers: http://www.parcconline.org

Achieve the Core: http://achievethecore.org

Smarter Balanced Assessment Consortium: http://www.smarterbalanced.org

Common Core State Standards Initiative: www.corestandards.org

International Reading Association: www.reading.org

Project Gutenberg (free ebooks): www.gutenberg.org

Free Public Domain Audiobooks: https://librivox.org

Curriculum-Based Measurement: www.easycbm.com

Intervention Central: www.interventioncentral.org

Reading A–Z: http://www.readinga-z.com

Read, Write, Think: www.readwritethink.org

Read Works: www.readworks.org

## Literacy Experts

Fisher & Frey Literacy for Life: www.fisherandfrey.com

Fountas & Pinnell: www.resources.fountasandpinnell.com

Timothy Shanahan: www.shanahanonliteracy.com